D1402721

SECRET GARDENS

SECRET
GARDENS

CREATING ROMANTIC RETREATS

ALAN TOOGOOD

TRAFALGAR SQUARE INC., NORTH POMFRET, VERMONT

ACKNOWLEDGEMENTS

The publishers are grateful to the following for granting permission for reproduction of colour photographs: Michael Boys (p. 2); John Heseltine (pp. 7, 47, 50, 62, 63, 103, 111 & 115); Linda Burgess (p. 11); Jerry Harpur (pp. 15, 39, 59, 82, 83, 86, 118 & 119); Richard Balfour (pp. 19 & 26); Tania Midgeley (pp. 23 & 91); Bob Challinor (p. 31); Tessa Traeger (p. 38); Hugh Palmer (p. 46); Pamla Toler (pp. 71, 74, 79 & 107); and Garden & Landscape Pictures (p. 110). The photographs on pp. 42, 54, 55, 67, 70, 94, 95, 99 & 123 were taken by Bob Challinor; the photograph on p. 43 was taken by David Ward.

The photographs on p. 67 were taken at Clack's Farm, courtesy of Arthur Billitt and the photographs on pp. 11, 16, 30, 31 & 32 were taken at Turnpike Cottage, Wimborne, courtesy of Lys de Bray.

Figures 1–10 were drawn by Cynthia Pow and Figures 11–27 were drawn by Nils Solberg.

Frontispiece: The cool shady grotto was a favourite garden feature with the Victorians. This rather formal design acts as a focal point in this garden, being seen through an arch in a hedge.

© Ward Lock Ltd 1987

First published in the United States in 1988 by Trafalgar Square Inc., North Pomfret, Vermont 05053.

House editor Denis Ingram
Designed by Melissa Orrom

Text set in Garamond original
by Hourds Typographica, Stafford
Printed and bound in Spain by
Graficas Reunidas S.A.

Library of Congress Catalog Card Number: 8750732

ISBN 0-943955-01-7

CONTENTS

PREFACE

I like a garden which cannot be seen in one glance: an inviting garden, full of surprises at every turn, with many secluded areas for the enjoyment of plants and outdoor living.

This is the theme of *Secret Gardens*, which suggests how you can create small gardens within the garden, each with its particular atmosphere. I want to bring romance back into gardening, as it seems to have been lost in recent times, so many of my secret gardens have imaginative and picturesque features which create a romantic atmosphere.

In these pages you will find the cool shady grotto; a woodland glade with dappled sunlight; the courtyard, a cool intimate retreat with the restful sound of a sparkling fountain; a terrace for entertaining your guests on a warm summer's evening; old-fashioned herb and rose gardens, delightfully fragrant on a warm summer's day; a secluded seat beneath an arbour, draped with scented climbers; a little chamomile lawn which scents the air at every step; the intimate patio for outdoor living; a scented garden whose plants attract clouds of butterflies; the conservatory or garden room, where exotic flowers and foliage can be enjoyed with a drink after dinner; cool peaceful water gardens; a children's garden which stimulates imaginary adventure.

Other features are more down to earth but nevertheless very attractive ideas for secret areas: a wild-life garden; a walled garden for choice tender plants; a heather and conifer garden for year-round colour; a rock garden; island beds for colourful hardy perennials; and more besides.

Sprinkled throughout the book are interesting historical facts which show that many garden features are far from new: indeed some were developed by ancient civilizations.

I take a look at what an old established garden has to offer in the way of secluded areas and how to adapt any existing features; and suggest how to divide a new or relatively featureless plot to create secret areas (considering gardens of various shapes and sizes).

Further chapters reveal how to make or plant the many features described, from walls, paths, pools and pergolas, to shrubs, trees, hedges and many other plants.

Having created attractive features in our secret gardens we should not neglect them, so the book is rounded off with a chapter on care and maintenance.

A.T.

Opposite: A pool and fountain are almost essential features in the cool courtyard and the more ornate they are the better.

1
SECRET GARDENS PAST AND PRESENT

The idea of enclosing gardens or areas around dwelling places, and of enclosing parts of gardens, stems from ancient civilizations. The ancient Egyptians, Greeks and Romans, for instance, made use of walls and hedges; and cool secluded courtyards were a feature of Greek and Roman houses, decorated with trees in containers, statues and pools.

In Europe, particularly in medieval times, enclosures were primarily for defence, as in the walled castles and, later, fortified manor houses with high walls and moats, of the upper classes. Often inside these walls were utility gardens providing herbs and food crops.

The evolution of villages saw houses enclosed with walls and fences, both for protection from intruders and from grazing animals.

Monasteries were enclosed within high walls to provide seclusion and often included leisure and utility gardens and fish ponds. The fish were used as a source of food by the monks.

Later still, gardens were enclosed for neatness and formality, as with Tudor gardens, which often featured formal courtyards.

TYPES OF ENCLOSURE

In medieval times land was often enclosed with wattle fences, and later with wooden palings. Wood and iron railings were extensively used from the Middle Ages.

Walls have been built since ancient times: the size and height used to surround the property usually depended on the lawlessness of the surrounding countryside. Earliest walls were made of stone, but later bricks were often used. Size of walls was reduced as law and order prevailed. Eventually viewing gaps were left in walls so that one could see the surrounding countryside. By the early eighteenth century walls around many large gardens and estates were demolished, following the new fashion in landscaping whereby the garden was made to blend with the countryside. There was indeed quite a revolt against enclosures. Ha-has or ditches surrounded gardens to keep out farm animals.

The so-called 'landscape era' came to an end in the early nineteenth century when the Industrial Revolution resulted in smaller properties.

Trimmed hedges have been used for centuries and are really a form of topiary which was practised by the Romans. Clipped hedges were particularly popular in the Tudor period and indeed since then have probably never lost their popularity.

In the fifteenth and sixteenth centuries gardens were often enclosed and divided with wooden arbours, or long tunnels, which supported climbing plants. They disappeared in the eighteenth century with the advent of the 'landscape revolution'. By the nineteenth century there was tremendous interest in training fruits, which necessitated the building of internal walls and other supporting structures. One type of wall often used was the serpentine or crinkle-crankle wall which created sheltered positions for the fruits.

——— *WHY SECRET GARDENS?* ———

As already mentioned, gardens have for centuries been divided into various parts for different uses. In the past this was mainly for practical purposes but today the idea of dividing a garden to create secret areas is for aesthetic reasons: so that you cannot see the entire garden in one glance, to create elements of surprise, and to provide pleasant secluded areas for the enjoyment of plants and outdoor living.

The boundaries of gardens today are often surrounded by walls, fences or hedges to create privacy in the garden as a whole, so I will not dwell on this aspect. There is no doubt that the British do like their privacy—indeed, the modern idea of open-plan front gardens has never caught on in this country. Many people who have open-plan front gardens really wish they could enclose them!

Secret gardens—or gardens within gardens—open up a wide range of possibilities for features. Each little garden can be quite different from the others, so that there is a surprise at every turn.

Secret gardens can, if desired, be romantic gardens. I feel that romance needs to be brought back into gardening and therefore it is the essence of my book. The small secluded gardens described have imaginative features which create a particular atmosphere. Many have been enjoyed by garden owners over the centuries, like the cool grotto, much loved by the Victorians; the arbour or shady recess which stems from the Middle Ages; the sunken garden of the Tudor period; water gardens which, surprisingly perhaps, were developed by the ancient Egyptians and Romans; herb gardens, with their medieval atmosphere; the courtyard garden, a cool, intimate retreat popular since ancient Greek and Roman periods, as is the terrace; and, beloved by the Victorians, the conservatory and the formal rose garden. These, and others are what I consider to be romantic gardens.

Other ideas are more modern and less romantic, like the wildlife garden, heather and conifer beds and island beds of perennials. Although rock gardens have been built since the eighteenth century it is really only since the middle of the nineteenth century that they have been attractively planted with alpines. Today the rock garden is a highly popular garden feature.

Large gardens and estates of the past often had a walled garden and indeed some of these still exist. They have their own warm micro-climate, ideal for the cultivation of many plants.

These and other features will, I hope, inspire you to create some attractive hideaway gardens.

2
NATURAL SECRET GARDENS

If you take over an old, established garden, one which was originally planned or well laid out, you may find that there are lots of little hidden areas that could be adapted to create attractive, secluded features. Really, people who take on old gardens have an easier task ahead of them than those with new gardens or other relatively featureless plots (see Chapter 3), even though they may have the task of taming a jungle. Certainly they will not have to wait for years for a mature effect.

So, presuming you have a rather neglected, perhaps overgrown garden, I suggest that you carefully consider every area and plant before you start clearing and thinning. It is all too easy to become carried away when faced with an overgrown plot and clear it to such an extent that the whole garden becomes visible in one glance.

Let's take a look at what an old overgrown garden may have to offer.

There may be groups of mature shrubs creating hidden areas which could be turned into delightful features, such as a winter garden with winter-flowering plants and shrubs with coloured bark. Very secluded parts may be ideal for creating sitting areas, especially if they receive plenty of sun and are sheltered from the wind. A scented garden is another idea for a sunny sheltered spot as in these conditions plant scents are most pronounced.

If the group of shrubs is rather rough and would be better grubbed out—think again, expecially if you have children. Could this be turned into a children's play area? Children love jungle-like conditions as they stimulate the imagination.

If there is a group of trees in the garden then you are indeed fortunate, for this area could be turned into a woodland garden, complete with a wood-land glade. If the soil is acid you could have an exotic woodland containing rhododendrons, camellias and other choice plants; if it is alkaline how about an English woodland with bluebells, primroses and other native plants?

Coming back to children, a large mature tree might be ideal for build-ing a tree house. Tree houses are not often seen today, but they were once popular with adults as well as children. Don't forget that if there is an old garden shed this could perhaps be used by your children as a play cabin.

Too many gardens are flat, so if you have a bank then you are indeed fortunate—make the most of it. How about a rock garden and maybe a grotto—a little picturesque cave? Maybe a waterfall, too, coursing through the rock garden? A rock garden can be planted with alpines, or left com-pletely natural, with grass between the rock outcrops.

Other undulations of the land could be adapted. For instance, if the ground falls away from the house then you may have the ideal site for creating a terrace, maybe looking down on to a parterre, a group of small geometric beds forming a pattern.

A low-lying area could be turned into one of several different features. If it is a definite hollow or deep depression why not consider turning it into a

sunken garden? This could be quite a formal feature, perhaps with rose beds and a formal pool with a fountain. Or you could turn the hollow into a pool. If the ground lies very wet you have the ideal site for a bog garden—there are lots of attractive bog and moisture-loving plants which you could grow.

While on the subject of water, you will indeed be fortunate if you have a natural stream running through the garden. This could be turned into a marvellous feature by planting the banks with bog and moisture-loving plants.

Conservation of native plants and fauna concerns many people today, so much so that they are creating wildlife habitats in their gardens. If you have a neglected area why not consider turning it—or part of it—into a wild-life garden? It may already have a number of native plants which would attract butterflies and other insects, birds and so on. An area of long grass could be turned into a wild-flower meadow; a bit of neglected woodland would be a haven for all sorts of creatures; while an old hedge, which may have reverted to the wild, containing native shrubs, trees and wild flowers, would provide nesting sites and food (in the form of berries and fruits) for birds. That patch of stinging nettles which you are threatening to spray with weedkiller is food for the caterpillars of several of our most attractive butter-flies. If it is well hidden from the rest of the garden then my advice is to leave it.

In the next chapter you will see that I have recommended creating focal

Statuary can be used as focal points in a garden to entice one to explore. This statue draws the eye to a tasteful planting of rhododendrons.

points to draw the eye to various parts of the garden. One is tempted to walk towards a focal point and on reaching it one should, ideally, suddenly come across a hidden area. If, therefore, parts of the garden are visible through, say, gaps in hedges, through groups of shrubs, or even through a wrought-iron gate in a wall, then make good use of these features. Create focal points which can be seen through the gaps—using, for instance, specimen shrubs or trees, statuary, urns etc.

If there are no views at all in the garden, then you should consider some clearing to open up vistas or long views, as I have described in the next chapter. Perhaps you could deliberately cut some gaps in hedges, or remove some of the shrubs from a large group so that you have tantalizing glimpses of the garden beyond, yet not destroying those secret, secluded areas.

Very often there are paved areas of some kind in old gardens and more often than not they are drab and uninteresting. Consider introducing carpeting plants into the gaps if it's 'crazy' or random-stone paving—far more interesting than the weeds that are likely to have taken over. Slabs can be removed here and there from areas of pre-cast concrete paving slabs and these little beds planted with suitable dwarf or prostrate plants. You may be able to cut similar beds in an area of concrete, or make it more interesting with a collection of stone sinks planted with alpines, or with groups of ornamental urns and pots.

3
STARTING FROM SCRATCH

Taking on a new garden or some other relatively featureless plot is probably more challenging than tackling a well-established garden which may already be divided into a number of smaller areas. You will also need some degree of patience for, depending on the types of screening used to create smaller intimate areas, it will take at least a few years to achieve an established atmosphere.

Exactly how you divide the plot will depend on its shape and size—it may be a long narrow garden, a small square plot so typical of modern town houses, or you may be lucky enough to have a fairly extensive or very large garden. There is no doubt that the first two examples are the most difficult to divide effectively and very careful thought needs to go into their planning. While we do not want the whole garden to be seen in one glance, at the same time we do not want to create a claustrophobic atmosphere. A garden should have views or vistas which draw the eye to various parts. This can give the impression that a garden is larger than it really is. It is a mistake to think that every part of a garden should be a secret secluded area. In a very small garden be content with only one or two secret areas.

A large garden is far more easily divided and there is less risk of making serious mistakes. One should aim for long vistas to draw the eye and at the ends of these there can be several or many secluded areas, or gardens within the garden. One should preserve the feeling of space in a large area—for example, a large lawn can create a feeling of spaciousness.

THE OVERALL PLAN

Each area or secret garden should be integrated into the overall plan of the garden—in other words, not isolated or 'out on a limb'. Areas should be linked together in some way. There are lots of ways of achieving this so let us consider them in some detail. In any one garden several of these ideas should be used, even if the plot is very small.

FOCAL POINTS

To my way of thinking, the easiest way of planning a garden from scratch is first to decide on a number of focal points. A focal point is an object or feature which draws the eye so that one is tempted to walk towards it and admire it more closely. It might be a specimen tree or shrub, or a piece of statuary, for example. On reaching the focal point you suddenly come across another part of the garden, hitherto hidden from view. Focal points, then, direct attention to various parts of the garden and they provide a sense of unity, linking the various parts or areas. Focal points can create a feeling of distance, too, for usually they are positioned at the ends of paths, at the far

end of a lawn, etc. Plenty of examples of focal points are shown in the accompanying drawings.

Once you have decided on focal points you can then proceed to divide the garden, confident that you will be preserving a sense of space and ensuring pleasing views. When you are physically laying out the garden you should endeavour to establish your focal points at a very early stage, especially if you are intending to use plants, for these need time to establish and grow into decent-sized specimens.

Needless to say, objects or plants for use as focal points need to be chosen with great care. First, they must be distinctive and secondly they must suit the size of the garden. In a large garden you may need something quite imposing while in a tiny garden more diminutive focal points are called for.

Hardware as focal points

Man-made objects are often used as focal points. Statuary has always been popular and is still in vogue. It can create a romantic atmosphere. Plenty of examples can be seen in garden centres for modest prices, but if you want something more up-market, or even antique, you should contact one of the specialist suppliers.

Statuary is available in stone, simulated stone, bronze, lead and even fibreglass. There is something to suit all pockets. There are human figures, animals, birds and abstract works. The latter are probably more in keeping in ultra-modern gardens, while human figures, animals and birds look at

home in both country and town gardens. Bear in mind that white or light-coloured statuary shows up best, especially in a dark or shady corner, particularly if it is backed by shrubs with deep green foliage. Dark-coloured statuary should have a light-coloured background.

Urns and vases in classical styles make excellent focal points in both formal and informal gardens and help to create a romantic atmosphere. They vary greatly in size so are suitable for all gardens. I am particularly fond of urns and vases in terracotta, which has a lovely 'warm' orangey colour. They are also available in light-coloured simulated stone and even in lead, the latter being very expensive. Again make sure that urns and vases have a background which shows them to advantage. Of course, they can be used as containers for plants, but I prefer, when using them as focal points, not to plant them for they are attractive objects in their own right.

Sundials have always been popular as focal points and so, too, have stone bird-baths. The latter is practical as well as having aesthetic qualities. They look particularly attractive in formal rose gardens, positioned so that they can be seen through a gap in the surrounding hedge (rose gardens are traditionally surrounded by hedges – for example, yew or holly).

A formal circular or square pool with a sparkling fountain makes a superb focal point – moving water certainly attracts the eye. I think that this feature is more suited to a formal garden, rather than an informal or country garden, as a fountain is really an artificial type of feature. It seems that fountains were first used by the Romans and the idea was developed in Renaissance Italy and ultimately all over Europe. Can there be a more romantic feature than a fountain? A pool and fountain can be used, for example, as a focal point in a courtyard garden, perhaps glimpsed through a wrought-iron gate, in the corner or centre of a small garden, maybe framed by an archway, or as the centrepiece of a sunken garden or rose garden, again making sure it can be seen through a gap in a hedge or other screen.

An ornamental garden seat is a useful focal point, especially a white-painted cast-iron one in a traditional style: an excellent choice for a country garden. There are plenty of modern styles available for more formal gardens. A seat can be backed by a hedge or wall to emphasize it and perhaps to afford wind protection.

Although a white-painted wrought-iron gazebo is often placed in an intimate, secluded part of the garden for use as a sitting area, it also makes a superb focal point in the medium-sized or large garden. It can support climbing plants such as roses and clematis and should be given a background of dark green shrubs or conifers.

Also in the larger garden a circular greenhouse makes an attractive focal point, especially if it is painted white. In it can be grouped a collection of colourful pot plants. Place it on a circular paved area. A greenhouse should be positioned in one of the sunniest parts of the garden.

Plants as focal points

Plants of distinctive shape can be used as focal points but of course they do not give the desired result immediately – unless you are prepared to spend money on semi-mature specimens.

There is a wide range of plants to choose from, particularly among the conifers, many of which are shaped like cones or pillars. Golden conifers

Fig. 2. This long narrow garden has been divided by means of trellis screens and screen-block walling. Note the long vista through the two arches in the trellis screens, and the shorter vista through the wrought-iron gate in the wall, each terminated by a focal point – a statue and an urn.

show up particularly well but bluish or greyish conifers are useful, too, especially for providing a sense of distance. Conifers range from dwarfs for small gardens to large specimens for bigger gardens.

The following are among my favourites for focal points. Of the golden conifers I can particularly recommend *Chamaecyparis lawsoniana* 'Lanei', which forms a broad cone 10–15 m in height with a spread of 5 m (33–50 by 16 ft); *Cupressus macrocarpa* 'Goldcrest', cone-shaped, 10 m in height with a spread of 3 m (33 by 10 ft); the golden Irish yew, *Taxus baccata* 'Fastigiata Aurea', a narrow column 4–5 m (14–16 ft) in height; *Thuja occidentalis* 'Rheingold', a broad cone or dome shape, height and spread about 3 m (10 ft), although slow growing; and the golden pfitzer juniper, *Juniperus* × *media* 'Pfitzerana Aurea', with a flattish habit, forming layers of horizontal branches, 1 m in height by 3 m across (3 by 10 ft).

Of the greyish or bluish conifers I can recommend *Chamaecyparis lawsoniana* 'Pembury Blue' which makes a silvery blue, broad cone 7–10 m in height with a spread of 2.4 m (23–33 by 8 ft); *Chamaecyparis pisifera* 'Boulevard', a broad cone of silvery blue, 3–4 m (10–13 ft) in height and spread, but slow growing; the Irish juniper, *Juniperus communis* 'Hibernica', a grey-green column 4.5–6 m (15–20 ft) in height; *Juniperus virginiana* 'Skyrocket', a very narrow bluish grey column 6–7 m (20–23 ft) in height; Koster's blue spruce, *Picea pungens* 'Koster', a broad silvery blue cone 7–10 m (23–33 ft) in height with a spread of about one-third of this; *Picea pungens* 'Moerheimii', similar in habit and size but blue-grey in colour; and the grey *Juniperus squamata* 'Meyeri,' whose branches are held out at a 45-degree angle, 3 m (10 ft) in height and spread.

Some of the Japanese maples, varieties of *Acer palmatum*, make excellent focal points, especially in a natural part of the garden or in a woodland area. They like sheltered conditions. Most have a somewhat mushroom-shaped habit of growth and all are deciduous, so they only provide impact in the spring, summer and early autumn. Height is up to 4.5 m (15 ft) and spread 2.4 m (8 ft). Good varieties are 'Atropurpureum' with bronze-red leaves, and 'Dissectum Atropurpureum' in a similar colour but with finely cut foliage. The slow-growing *Acer japonicum* 'Aureum' also makes a superb focal point with its yellow foliage which turns crimson in autumn. Height is up to 6 m (20 ft) with a spread of 2.4 m (8 ft).

Weeping trees can also be recommended as focal points, and ideal for creating a sense of distance is the deciduous silver-leaved pear, *Pyrus salicifolia* 'Pendula'. It has silvery willow-like leaves and a height and spread of about 4.5 m (15 ft).

Fastigiate or narrow columnar trees make dramatic focal points. There are lots of small ornamental trees with this habit of growth, but for the larger garden I can recommend the Dawyck beech, *Fagus sylvatica* 'Dawyck', which grows to over 18 m (60 ft) in height. There is a golden-leaved form, 'Dawyck Gold', and a purple form, 'Dawyck Purple', both of medium height—10–18 m (33–60 ft). Beeches are, of course, deciduous but even in winter these distinctive trees are still able to create impact.

A dramatic golden-leaved deciduous tree which I can recommend is the round-headed *Robinia pseudoacacia* 'Frisia' with rich golden yellow foliage from spring to autumn. It grows to a height of at least 9 m (30 ft) with a spread of about 3 m (10 ft).

A secluded seat reached by a delightful path which is planted with scented thymes and other carpeting plants. The path is flanked on each side with dwarf lavender hedges.

Among the hardy perennials there is no finer plant for use as a focal point than the pampas grass, *Cortaderia selloana*, with glaucous arching leaves and huge silvery plumes of flowers in late summer/autumn on towering 2.4 m (8 ft) stems. The foliage is evergreen and produced in huge clumps. The plumes need a dark background to show them off. The variety 'Sunningdale Silver' has larger plumes than the species and they are white. For limited space try 'Pumila,' just 1.2–1.8 m (4–6 ft) high, which is also more compact. Many people use pampas grass as a focal point in a lawn.

PATHS

Various areas or parts of the garden can of course be linked by paths. In a large garden the areas may be separated by expanses of lawn. In this situation it is a nice idea to run paths across a lawn, ideally in the form of stepping

Fig. 3. *In this long narrow garden the vistas run diagonally across it, each terminating in a focal point. This gives the impression that the garden is wider than it really is. Again trellis screens with arches have been used, but angled diagonally across the garden.*

stones, to link one area with another. Wherever possible paths should be winding and should certainly disappear from view in order to create elements of surprise. Focal points can be set at the ends of paths, or wherever a path changes direction. Examples of this technique will be found in the accompanying drawings. Paths should of course lead to definite places of interest – try to create a 'surprise' at the end of each.

In a small garden it may not be feasible to have paths as such, but each part can be linked with areas of paving, perhaps, or with gravel.

STEPS

Wherever possible make use of steps as an entrance to a secret garden, particularly if you have a garden on different levels. For some reason which I cannot really explain steps always seem to beckon one to explore further! An obvious place to feature steps is at the entrance to a sunken garden. Steps need not be difficult to construct, either; they can be as simple as log risers held in place with wooden stakes.

GAPS, ARCHES AND GATES

Hedges, trelliswork, fences, walls and other screens used to divide a garden can be provided with gaps which are used as entrances to secret gardens, as shown in the accompanying drawings. Try to provide a focal point that can be seen from the outside, to entice one inside.

You can also see from my drawings that I am very fond of arches and these could be incorporated into gaps in hedges, fences, etc. An arch makes an excellent framework for the internal focal point. An arch can be formed from the hedging plants, or ready-made timber or steel arches can be bought. You can train climbing plants over these.

Gaps and arches give tantalizing glimpses of the garden beyond, encouraging one to explore further. A tall wrought-iron gate, say in the wall of a courtyard, has the same effect. Again make sure there is a focal point that can be seen through it—in the case of a courtyard, perhaps a statue, or a pool with a fountain.

Some gardens I have visited feature solid gates in walls but I feel these are perhaps better suited to large gardens. They certainly have the desired effect of encouraging one to explore—how can one resist finding out what lies beyond?

DIVIDING A GARDEN

What we use to divide a garden, to create our secret areas, will depend on the size and style of the garden. For example, in a small plot it makes no sense to use very wide hedges or screens for they would take up too much space. In a country garden you may want to use informal-looking screens, while in a modern town garden formality can prevail. One must consider the cost, too. Walls are far and away the most expensive screens; fences (especially pre-fabricated panels) and trelliswork screens are cheaper, and so, too, are hedging plants. If you want a quick effect, then, the choice will be between walls, fences and trelliswork screens. Hedges or other living screens obviously take some years to screen parts of the garden effectively. Growth rates differ, though; some hedging plants are very fast growing while others are painfully slow. Let us, then, consider in some detail the screening materials available.

HEDGES

There is no doubt that hedges are very popular for dividing gardens, possibly because they are cheaper than many other forms of screening. Also, many people do like living screens as they make marvellous backgrounds for other plants.

All hedging plants should be evergreen (or at least retain dead leaves through the winter) if they are to be effective all the year round.

Basically there are two forms of hedges: the formal and the informal. The formal hedge is clipped to a regular shape, generally a wedge shape, broad at the base and gradually tapering to about half (or less) of the basal width to the top. These hedges need regular clipping to keep them looking neat and tidy. Formal hedges are ideal for more formal gardens, although they are often used, too, in country gardens. If you have only a very small plot then hedging might not be a good choice, for although hedges can be trained into quite narrow shapes they may still take up too much space.

Informal hedges are allowed to grow naturally—in other words, they are not trimmed to a regular shape. Often flowering or berrying plants are used to create colourful hedges. Informal hedges can become very wide—2.4 m (8 ft) or more, so should only be considered where space is not limited. They are most in keeping in large country gardens.

One often thinks only in terms of planting hedging plants in straight lines, but a hedge does not have to be straight. Some marvellous effects can be created with curved hedges, for example, as shown in some of my drawings. L-shaped hedges are useful, too, for creating secluded areas.

To screen parts of the garden effectively hedges need to be about 1.8 m (6 ft) high. Informal hedges grow to at least this height, often more. I would not advise letting a formal hedge grow much higher than this, as it will become difficult to cut.

Tall screens might be useful if you have a very large garden. Conifers are often used: the plants are given slightly wider spacings than for hedging and allowed to grow to their natural heights. An example is shown in the illustration on p.35.

Let us now consider some plants which can be used for hedges and screens.

Plants for formal hedges

Buxus sempervirens (box)   Popular hedging plant with small rounded deep green leaves. Grows well on chalky soils. Moderately slow growing. Makes a very dense hedge if regularly clipped.

Carpinus betulus (hornbeam)   Although it is deciduous, hornbeam holds on to its dead, golden brown leaves all winter. A fast grower. Good on chalky and clay soil and in exposed sites.

Chamaecyparis lawsoniana 'Green Hedger' (Lawson's cypress)   A conifer with dense sprays of deep green foliage. Excellent for clay soils and exposed sites. Quite a fast grower.

× *Cupressocyparis leylandii* (Leyland cypress)   This is the fastest-growing hedging conifer—it can make up to 90 cm (3 ft) of growth in a year. It is clothed with sprays of dark green foliage. There is also a golden-leaved form which makes a bright screen. Thrives on chalky soils and tolerant of exposed sites. Good by the sea, too.

Cupressus macrocarpa (Monterey cypress)   This is another fast-growing conifer, but not so fast as the Leyland cypress. The bright green foliage is carried in sprays. Only suitable for mild and coastal gardens.

A secluded seat in a shady recess or arbour, in this instance built of natural stone. Climbers over the arbour help to provide shade.

Euonymus japonicus   This has shiny, deep green, oval leaves and grows quite fast. It can be grown in shade, in polluted areas and by the sea.

Fagus sylvatica (beech)   A popular deciduous hedging plant that holds on to its dead, golden brown leaves all winter. Attractive in spring as the young leaves are bright green. Quite a fast grower. Thrives in chalky soils and tolerates exposed windy sites.

Ilex aquifolium and cultivars (holly)   Dark green prickly leaves; forms a really dense hedge if regularly clipped. Slow grower. Grows well in clay soil and tolerates coastal exposure.

Ligustrum ovalifolium (privet)   A widely used hedging plant with small deep green oval leaves, but not one that I would highly recommend as it needs very frequent clipping and is inclined to die out in patches (it's highly prone to honey fungus). The cultivar 'Aureum' is the well-known golden privet with bright yellow foliage. Privet is a fast grower and grows literally anywhere.

Lonicera nitida (Chinese honeysuckle)   A popular hedging plant with very tiny oval dark green leaves. It's a fast grower but like privet is inclined to die out in places. Useful for chalky and clay soils.

Prunus laurocerasus (cherry laurel)   This has very large oval shiny deep green leaves and is a fast grower. Its cultivar 'Rotundifolia' can be especially recommended. Not too happy on chalky soils or in exposed areas.

Prunus lusitanica (Portugal laurel)   This has large, oval, dark green shiny foliage. A fast grower. Tolerates cold exposed areas, shade and chalky soils.

Taxus baccata (yew)   Once this was an extremely popular hedging plant, being widely used for formal hedging: it's amenable to training into all kinds of shapes and is certainly the best subject for topiary. However, due to its very slow growth it has lost some of its popularity in this age of 'instant gardening'. But it is an excellent hedging plant, forming a dense deep green hedge. It will tolerate shade, exposed windy sites and chalky and clay soils. It is the traditional hedge for enclosing a rose garden and it makes a marvellous background for statuary.

Thuja occidentalis (white cedar)   A conifer with deep green foliage carried in sprays. It is quite a fast grower, and although it can be grown almost anywhere it does need good drainage.

Thuja plicata 'Atrovirens' (western red cedar)   Another conifer with bright green shiny foliage carried in sprays. It also is quite a fast grower and will tolerate clay and chalky soils. I particularly like this conifer as it has aromatic foliage, very noticeable when crushed – it has a fruity scent.

Plants for informal hedges

Berberis darwinii (barberry)   Produces yellow flowers in spring set against prickly deep green leaves. Moderately fast grower, doing particularly well in chalky soils.

Berberis × stenophylla (barberry)   In spring deep yellow flowers are produced against a background of deep green foliage. Arching habit of growth and a moderately fast grower. Grows well on chalk. This is undoubtedly one of the most popular shrubs for informal hedges.

Cotoneaster lacteus   This shrub produces red berries in autumn/winter set against medium green foliage. Moderately fast grower. Grows well in coastal gardens and in chalky and clay soils.

Elaeagnus pungens 'Maculata'   This fairly slow-growing shrub makes a very bright hedge with its gold-splashed leaves. Another good subject for coastal gardens.

Escallonia rubra macrantha   In summer this is covered with rose-red flowers. It is quite a fast grower and an excellent choice for coastal gardens and mild areas inland. Grows well on chalky soils.

Pyracantha atalantioides (firethorn)   Carries heavy crops of red berries in the autumn. Spiny habit, forming a thick hedge. A fast grower. Very adaptable – grows anywhere.

Rhododendron ponticum   Trusses of mauve flowers in early summer. A slow grower, needing acid (lime-free) soil. Suitable for a position in partial shade. This is a very tough shrub.

Viburnum tinus (laurustinus)   Produces a long succession of white flowers in winter and spring, set against large deep green leaves. Can be grown anywhere and is extremely good for chalky soils.

Plants for tall screens

Chamaecyparis lawsoniana (Lawson's cypress)   A conifer with dense sprays of medium green foliage. Quite a fast grower and excellent for clay soils and exposed sites.

× *Cupressocyparis leylandii*, *Cupressus macrocarpa* and *Thuja plicata* also make excellent tall screens – for details see Plants for formal hedges, p.22.

Fig. 4. Opposite: *Here is an unusual but attractive way of dividing a long narrow garden – curved hedges have been used. This is a particularly suitable idea for a country garden. Again, by means of focal points, the eye is lead diagonally across the garden, giving the impression of greater width.*

This is everyone's dream – a natural stream running through the garden. Here, the banks are planted with purple aubrieta and white perennial candytuft. Fortunately artificial streams are not too difficult to construct.

GROUPS OF SHRUBS

Groups of ornamental shrubs can be arranged to form screens and they have a far more informal appearance than formal hedges and even informal hedges. They are not planted in rows, as are hedging plants, but in bold irregular groups. Groups of shrubs are particularly recommended for country or natural gardens, where informality is the keynote.

Obviously you want quick-growing shrubs and they should ultimately be high enough to make effective screens – that is, at least 1.8 m (6 ft) in height. Aim to have a good mixture of evergreen and deciduous subjects, flowering, foliage and berrying kinds. The following should fit the bill.

Aesculus parviflora (horse chestnut) A bushy deciduous shrub to about 2.4 m (8 ft), spreading by suckers. Generally good autumn leaf colour and erect panicles of white flowers in mid-summer.

Arundinaria japonica (bamboo) Long broad deep green leaves, which are evergreen, carried on canes at least 3 m (10 ft) in height. Very vigorous, forming dense thickets. Needs plenty of space.

Berberis × *ottawensis* 'Purpurea' A very vigorous deciduous shrub, to at least 2.4 m (8 ft), with quite large oval leaves, rich purple in colour. Pale yellow flowers in spring.

Buddleia globosa (orange ball tree)   An extremely vigorous evergreen or semi-evergreen shrub to about 3 m (10 ft) in height. It produces masses of orange-yellow ball-shaped flowers in spring and early summer.

Corylus maxima 'Purpurea' (purple-leaf filbert)   This deciduous shrub has quite large rounded leaves which are rich purple in colour. It will attain a height of over 3 m (10 ft).

Cotoneaster 'Cornubia'   This is a semi-evergreen cotoneaster noted for its incredibly heavy crops of large red berries in the autumn. It will attain a height of at least 3 m (10 ft).

Forsythia 'Lynwood'   This is one of the most popular varieties of forsythia, and rightly so, for in spring it is laden with large brilliant yellow flowers which are conspicuous from a great distance. It is a vigorous grower and can attain a height of at least 1.8 m (6 ft).

Lonicera tatarica 'Hack's Red' (shrubby honeysuckle)   This is a vigorous deciduous shrub attaining a height of around 2.4 m (8 ft). It is not too well known but worth growing for its masses of rose pink flowers which are produced in late spring or early summer.

Philadelphus 'Virginal' (mock orange)   This is deservedly one of the most popular of the mock oranges. A deciduous shrub of over 3 m (10 ft) in height, it bears in early summer masses of double, pure white, highly fragrant flowers.

Pyracantha (firethorn)   These evergreen shrubs are very popular on account of their heavy crops of berries in autumn. There are several very good kinds, including *P. atalantioides*, scarlet berries, over 3 m (10 ft) high; 'Buttercup', deep yellow berries, at least 2.4 m (8 ft) high; *P. coccinea* 'Lalandei', orange-red berries; 'Golden Charmer', orange-yellow berries; 'Mohave', orange-red fruits; 'Orange Charmer', large deep orange berries; and *P. rogersiana* 'Flava', bright yellow berries. All grow over 3 m (10 ft) high.

Rhamnus alaterna 'Argenteovariegata' (buckthorn)   An evergreen shrub of at least 2.4 m (8 ft) in height with leaves variegated green, grey and creamy white. Vigorous bushy habit.

Ribes odoratum (golden currant)   This makes a change from the ubiquitous flowering currant (*Ribes sanguineum*). It is a deciduous shrub to at least 1.8 m (6 ft) in height and in mid-spring produces golden yellow scented flowers. The shiny leaves take on brilliant autumn tints.

Sambucus nigra 'Aurea' (golden elder)   This adaptable deciduous shrub has pinnate golden yellow leaves. It attains a height of 1.8–2.4 m (6–8 ft).

Spiraea veitchii   A deciduous shrub with arching branches, carrying in early to mid-summer masses of white flowers. It attains a height of over 3 m (10 ft).

Stranvaesia davidiana   This is a cotoneaster-like evergreen shrub of vigorous upright habit which produces clusters of crimson berries in the autumn, set against deep green foliage. It attains a height of over 3 m (10 ft).

Syringa × *josiflexa* 'Bellicent' (lilac)   This one makes a change from the common lilac (*Syringa vulgaris*). It has huge panicles of fragrant pink flowers in late spring and early summer, set against deep green foliage. It is a deciduous shrub, attaining a height of over 3 m (10 ft).

Viburnum opulus 'Notcutt's Variety' (guelder rose)   This has large white hydrangea-like flowers in early summer followed by red berries. Also good autumn leaf colour. It is a large shrub, growing to over 3 m (10 ft) in height.

Fig. 5. *A small, square, pocket-handkerchief garden partially screened with trellis panels which support climbing plants. Even in this small garden there is still a long view or vista, through the arch to the urn at the far end of the garden.*

Viburnum rhytidophyllum This viburnum is noted for its dramatic evergreen foliage. The long shiny leaves are deeply veined and covered with grey felt on the undersides. Creamy white flowers in flat heads are produced in late spring. It's a fast grower, attaining over 3 m (10 ft) in height.

WALLS

If the right style is chosen, walls are suitable for both town and country gardens. Due to their narrow width they are ideal, too, where space is limited, although do not overdo the use of solid walling in this situation as it can result in a closed-in effect. Instead consider openwork walling. Walling is expensive, of course, and may be cost-prohibitive on a large scale.

Walling is virtually essential if you want to create a courtyard garden. You may be able to make use of an existing boundary wall here, which will cut down the cost. There are various walling materials to choose from so let's take a closer look at them.

Bricks

Wherever possible try to choose bricks which match those of the house. Frost-resistant bricks are recommended for garden walls. There are lots of types to choose from, but for an aesthetically pleasing wall you should use facing bricks which have one or two attractive sides. They come in many colours and textures. Also suitable for garden walls are frost-proof calcium silicate (sand lime or flint lime) bricks, which are available in a wide choice of textures and colours.

For a country or cottage garden you may be able to obtain mellow, old-looking bricks.

A brick wall does not have to be solid; open brickwork walls are especially recommended in small areas–an open brickwork wall can be used around a patio, for example. Various types of brickwork are shown on p.87.

Ornamental concrete walling blocks

These are very popular for building garden walls. They are about brick size and available in various colours and textures, resembling natural stone. A good choice for country and cottage gardens.

Concrete screen blocks

These are large precast concrete blocks which have an openwork pattern. Screen-block walling is very popular, particularly for surrounding patios. It gives effective screening without considerably reducing light and is a good choice for a small town garden; it looks out of place in a country garden. Like trelliswork, screenblock walling gives one tempting glimpses of the garden beyond and it makes an excellent support for climbing plants, which weave their way in and out of the openwork pattern.

FENCES

As with walls, fences should be carefully considered for screening in small gardens for, being solid, they can also create a claustrophobic effect. Where there is plenty of space, though, fencing can be a reasonably economic method of dividing a garden.

As with hedging and walls, fencing should be about 1.8 m (6 ft) high to be effective. Do not think that it always has to be erected in a straight line–it can be curved or angled as desired, particularly if prefabricated panels are used. The type of fencing chosen should suit the style of garden so let us take a look at the various materials available.

Lapped or interwoven panels

This is one of the most popular types of fencing, being made from larch or pine, which may be lapped (overlapping) or interwoven. Panels can be bought in a good range of sizes. Prefabricated panels look good in both town and country gardens.

Wattle panels

Wattle fencing panels are made from hazelwood, which is closely woven. It is an economical form of fencing and looks particularly good in country or cottage gardens.

Close-boarded timber
This type of fencing is constructed on site, generally by a specialist. It is probably the most expensive form of fencing and is made from vertical or horizontal boards in hardwood or softwood, the former having a very long life. Close-boarded timber fencing looks particularly good in a modern setting, although it would not seem out of place in a country garden.

Ranch-type fencing
This is a very modern-looking type of fencing which is often used in town gardens. It consists of horizontal bars of timber (for example, pine), or PVC, with gaps between them. Timber ranch-type fencing is generally painted white. As you can partially see through this type of fencing, it is particularly recommended for smaller gardens where prevention of that boxed-in effect is all-important. It looks particularly effective when draped with colourful climbing plants such as roses and clematis.

Trelliswork screens
There is no doubt in my mind that trelliswork screens make the perfect dividers for small gardens for they do not seriously reduce light; nor do they result in a boxed-in effect. They take up minimum space and make perfect supports for climbing plants.

Trellis can be bought in prefabricated panels which come in a range of sizes. They may be made of larch, pine or cedarwood, the latter having the longest life. One has a choice of square or diamond pattern. There are one or two companies in Britain who specialize in traditional designs, some of which have fancy or attractively shaped tops. Trellis is an excellent choice for both town and country gardens.

A range of fencing materials is shown on p.92. Remember that prefabricated fencing panels and trelliswork screens are easily erected these days with the aid of metal post supports—there is no need to concrete posts into the ground. More of this in Chapter 6.

— THE SHAPE OF THE GARDEN —

Exactly how a garden is divided will depend on its shape and size. Very careful thought indeed has to go into dividing the long narrow garden, so typical of older town and city houses. The very small square plot, typical of modern town houses, needs careful consideration, too. If you have a medium-sized to large garden the task of dividing it becomes a lot easier, for you will not have the worry of creating a boxed-in-effect.

Always bear in mind when planning your garden that while you do not want the whole garden to be seen in one glance, at the same time you do not want to create a claustrophobic atmosphere. The garden should have some long views or vistas which draw the eye to various parts. And do not think that every part of the garden should be a secret, secluded area. A very small garden might have only one or two such areas, while a large garden provides scope for many. I have provided some ideas for dividing gardens of different shapes and sizes, as shown in the accompanying drawings, so let us consider these in some detail.

A LARGE RECTANGULAR GARDEN

A reasonably large rectangular garden, or even part of a very large garden, could be divided with staggered hedges as shown in Fig. 1. These provide an air of mystery and between each hedge a secret garden can be created. There is no need to use hedges, of course: the same effect can be created with walls or fences.

Note particularly that this garden has a long vista—the eye is drawn to the focal point at the far end, encouraging one to walk to it. But on the way there are all kinds of attractions on either side. Each 'section' could be provided with a focal point or distinctive feature to encourage one into it.

A waterfall cascading through a rock garden combine to make an attractive feature for a secluded area. The sound of moving water gives another dimension to the garden.

31

The walk to the far end should be kept completely open, free from plants etc, and ideally should be grassed, although a wide gravel walk would also be attractive. Note that one has tantalizing glimpses of tall plants between the hedges, which again tempt one to explore.

A LONG NARROW GARDEN

There is no doubt that this is one of the more difficult shapes to divide effectively, at the same time ensuring views or vistas.

Long narrow gardens are often found in towns and cities and one idea for such a garden is shown in Fig. 2. Here I have positioned the screens at right-angles across the garden. Each of the first two has a central opening, made more attractive by an arch, so creating a vista. Note the positioning of the two focal points which draw the eye. However you cannot see right to the end of the garden due to the fact that the opening in the screen at the far end has been set to one side, with a focal point to encourage one into this area.

As I did not want to create a closed-in feeling I have suggested trellis for the first two screens, clothed with climbing plants, which are trained over the arches. To provide variation I suggest a screen-block wall at the far end, with a wrought-iron gate set in the archway. If the garden is bounded by high brick walls the area at the far end could be turned into a delightful courtyard garden.

The paving which forms the patio could be extended into a path leading to the end of the garden.

So in this garden we have four secluded or secret areas which can be designed or planted as desired.

Another way of planning a long narrow garden is to have vistas which run diagonally across it, each terminating in a focal point, as shown in Fig. 3. This gives the impression that the garden is wider than it really is. Again I would suggest trellis screens with arches, but this time they are angled diagonally across the garden. Again the patio could be extended into a path which leads through the arches to a far corner of the garden. This plan also provides four secret areas, but remember that the number of screens used will be determined by the length of the garden. Do avoid having too many or you could end up with a series of little cells. It is far better to aim for space when designing a garden.

A completely different way of dividing a long narrow garden is shown in Fig. 4. The garden is divided by means of curved hedges. The idea is particularly suitable for a country garden, although there is no reason why it should not be used in a town or city garden.

Again, by means of focal points, the eye is lead diagonally across the garden, giving the impression of greater width. Note how the path zig-zags across the garden.

The number of hedges used will be determined by the length of the garden—again, do not be tempted to plant too many. Where space is limited I would suggest quite narrow formal hedges, as these take up far less space than informal hedges. These hedges, of course, make marvellous backgrounds for other plants, especially if you choose hedging plants with deep green foliage.

A SMALL SQUARE GARDEN

A small square 'pocket-handkerchief' garden, as found with modern houses in towns and cities, gives the most problems when it comes to creating intimate areas. I don't consider one can think in terms of completely enclosed areas in this situation, but rather try to partially screen parts of the plot, as shown in Fig. 5.

It is virtually essential to have openwork screens and so I have suggested erecting trellis panels: perhaps one of the fancy traditional styles of trellis, maybe painted white. An ornamental arch creates an additional feature and provides support for climbing plants. Once again, the number of screens used will be determined by the size of the plot. I feel that this approach makes a garden more intimate, yet at the same time ensures light airy conditions.

In a very small plot the ground is best paved, but you could leave spaces or beds in the paving for planting. In a paved garden you could also make good use of ornamental containers for plants.

Fig. 6. This medium-sized garden is divided by means of hedges and walls. Note how focal points draw the eye to the various secret areas. In this instance mainly distinctive plants have been used. Good use has been made of an existing high boundary wall to create a walled courtyard, by building a new L-shaped wall.

Note that even in this small garden there is a vista, terminated by a focal point, and framed by the arch.

The boundaries are usually determined by the builders but if you have a choice I would suggest white-painted ranch-type fencing, on which could be grown colourful climbers.

A MEDIUM-SIZED GARDEN

The gardens of older houses are often reasonably large—maybe up to a quarter of an acre—so creating a number of secret gardens is easier to achieve than with the average modern plot. There are numerous ways of laying out medium-sized gardens and one example is shown in Fig. 6, which consists of a combination of hedges and walls.

Part of the garden is divided by several hedges, arranged at right angles to each other, with gaps for access. Note how focal points draw the eye to these secret areas, seen through the gaps.

Good use has been made of an existing high boundary wall to create a walled courtyard, by building a new L-shaped wall. A high wrought-iron gate has been incorporated into the new wall to give a glimpse of the courtyard, the eye being drawn by a statue. A formal pool with a sparkling fountain has been included as this is an 'essential' feature of any courtyard, helping to create a cool atmosphere.

The pergola has been added purely for additional interest in this garden and of course makes an excellent support for a collection of climbing plants. By fixing one side of the pergola to the wall of the courtyard one can reduce the quantity of building materials needed.

This design is suitable for both town and country gardens. If you want a more informal design you could use groups of tall shrubs instead of hedges, but arranged in a similar way. Or have informal hedges, using flowering or berrying shrubs. This garden, then, has three reasonably large but very secluded areas yet at the same time gives a feeling of space.

A LARGE GARDEN

First, what do I mean by a large garden? Really I am thinking in terms of an acre and upwards. One tends to think that such gardens are few and far between, but during my travels I am constantly surprised by the number of people who have gardens of this size. Therefore, I make no apology for giving the large garden a fair bit of space in my book.

Generally I find that the owners of large gardens are very enthusiastic gardeners and possess a fair or very good knowledge of gardening. Most certainly seem to know what they are doing and on the whole their gardens are laid out attractively. So at the risk of teaching my grandmother to suck eggs, I put forward an idea for laying out a large area, featuring numerous secret gardens (see Fig. 7). This is a design for a country garden, as most large gardens are to be found in rural or semi-rural areas.

As you can see, it features hedges, living screens and groups of shrubs, all with gaps in them leading into secret parts. There is great scope in a large garden for curved hedges. In my plan they are formal hedges, but to keep work to a minimum you may wish to consider instead informal hedges,

Fig. 7. Opposite: *This is a design for a large country garden which features hedges, living screens and groups of shrubs, all helping to create numerous secret gardens. This garden also features a woodland glade – seen in the top right-hand corner.*

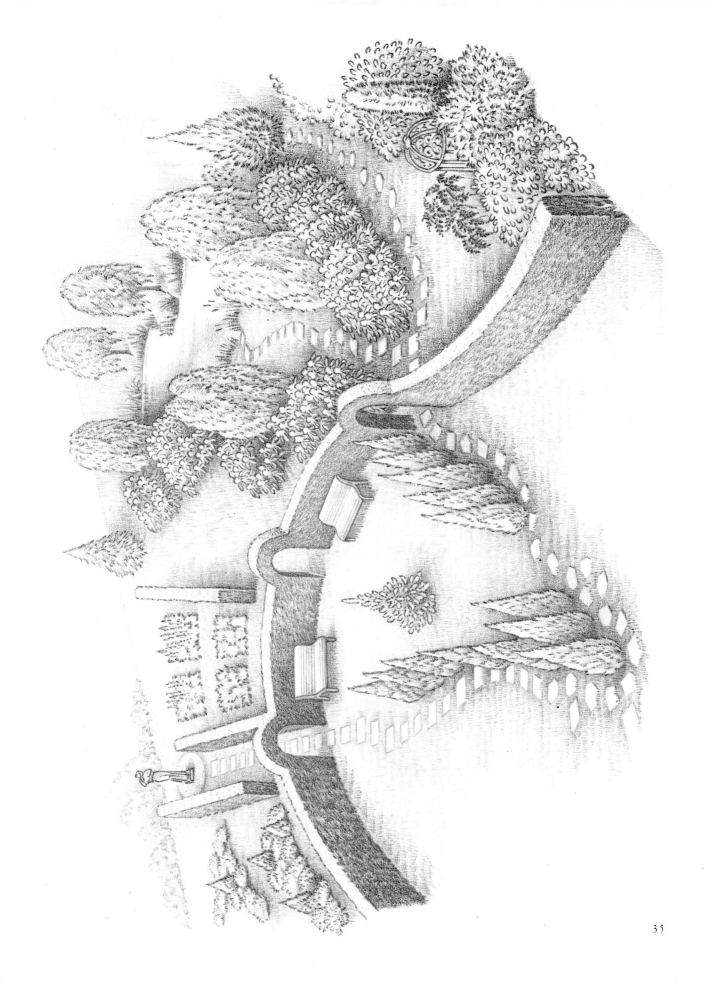

using flowering or berrying subjects. Once again I have made use of arches in the main hedge as I feel these give character to a garden. A focal point is visible through each arch. Note the two parallel hedges, each with a gap at one end, and a path between them. This is a useful means of dividing an area. The L-shaped screen is formed of conifers and helps to enclose a lawn, with a focal point in the middle, such as a specimen conifer.

This garden also features a woodland glade—you may be able to adapt existing woodland or a group of trees, or even start from scratch by planting your own. A path winds through the trees and on one of the bends is a focal point to encourage one to venture further. In this setting a Japanese maple would make an excellent focal point. Most of the woodland cannot be seen at a glance as groups of shrubs surround it.

Another area has also been planted with bold groups of shrubs, arranged in such a way that they create several secluded areas. One area has been planted as a winter garden, with shrubs and other plants which have winter interest and colour. It is in an out-of-the-way part of the garden as for most of the year it has little to offer in the way of colour. Close by, another area secluded by shrubs features a gazebo. This acts as a focal point and is also used as a sitting place, for quiet contemplation.

The various other secluded areas that the hedges and screens create can of course be devoted to ideas of your choice—for instance, you may want a heather and conifer garden, a herb garden and a long-grass area with wild flowers.

Note that there are no straight lines in this design, apart from three of the hedges, making it a truly informal garden. The winding paths, sometimes disappearing from view, encourage one to explore this garden.

4
ROMANTIC SECRET GARDENS

Having divided our garden into various areas we must now consider ideas for each. The more ideas that are put into a garden the more interesting it becomes. A very large garden offers the greatest scope, of course—it can be full of surprises—but even a small garden can have several quite different features.

If you want to give free rein to your imagination consider some of the ideas in this chapter. Some are extravagant or whimsical features, impractical but charming; and others are intended to create an intimate atmosphere. Some are a far cry from 'ordinary' garden features, little fantasy worlds, if you like. But all are guaranteed to please and surprise your visitors: and indeed give you endless enjoyment. Some of these ideas are not new, by any means, as they have been enjoyed by many garden owners over the centuries —indeed, since Roman times in some cases.

THE COOL SHADY GROTTO

A grotto is a small picturesque natural cave which makes an attractive retreat. Gardeners have been making artificial grottoes since Roman times and they were particularly popular with the Victorians. They would actually be excavated, say in a bank, or a structure would be built to resemble a cave. Often grottoes were lined internally with fanciful items like coloured glass, stones, shells, coloured rocks, crystals and so on. Some had internal water-falls, springs or streams.

I am not suggesting anything so ornate or ambitious for today's gardens, but I would recommend a small grotto, particularly as part of a rock garden built into a bank, as shown in Fig. 8. This is not intended to be an attractive retreat but rather a pleasing visual feature.

Ideas on how to build it will be found in Chapter 6, but basically you excavate a small cave in the bank, ensuring that the roof is reinforced, and it is lined and edged with natural rock, blending it into the rest of the rock garden.

A garden pool could be made in front of the grotto, extending it right to the back. To add movement and sound I suggest water dripping from the roof of the grotto into the pool. This is achieved by circulating the water in the pool by means of a small submersible pump. I have seen such a grotto in the garden of a friend and I can assure you it makes a most attractive and unusual feature. Of course, it should be well clothed with suitable plants and I would suggest ferns, with fresh green fronds, which will enjoy the cool conditions around the entrance to the grotto. There are many to choose from such as the hart's-tongue fern, *Phyllitis scolopendrium*, with bright green strap-shaped evergreen fronds. Even more attractive is the variety 'Crispum' whose edges are wavy and crinkled.

A tantalizing glimpse through an arch tempts one to explore this romantic secret garden.

Several of the dryopteris ferns would be suitable, too, such as *D. cristata*, the crested buckler fern, with pale green very feathery fronds (plant it at the edge of the pool, in boggy conditions); and *D. filix-mas*, the male fern, with lance-shaped deep green feathery fronds. For the edge of the pool I can recommend the royal fern, *Osmunda regalis*, which revels in moist conditions. It has 1.2 m (4 ft) high pea-green fronds which turn a delightful golden brown in autumn. The polypody, *Polypodium vulgare*, is a dwarf fern with bright green, drooping, pinnate fronds, ideal for planting at the top of the grotto. The soft shield fern, *Polystichum setiferum*, has medium green feathery fronds to a height of at least 60 cm (2 ft). If you have the space try

the variety 'Divisilobum' whose plume-like fronds spread to at least 1.2 m (4 ft).

The pool can be planted with aquatics, including waterlilies and marginal plants (see Water Gardens, p.55) and stocked with fish, provided it receives sun for a good part of the day. Aquatics do not thrive in shady pools.

This brick patio could not be more secluded as it is surrounded by tall yew hedges. Potted topiary specimens, formed of box, make unusual but highly attractive features (garden designers: Hillier & Hilton).

A WOODLAND GLADE

If you have the space a woodland glade can make a picturesque feature, perhaps most suited to a country garden, particularly in a naturally wooded area. A glade is an open space in woodland and I suggest this is achieved with a reasonably broad path meandering through the trees. Each side of the woodland can be planted with shade-loving plants of your choice.

Of course, if you have an area of natural woodland, or even a group of well-established trees, then it is a comparatively easy matter to create a woodland garden. Some thinning of trees may be needed, of course, both to create a glade and to ensure dappled rather than heavy shade in the rest of the woodland.

On the other hand you may need to start from scratch by planting your own woodland. Silver birches, *Betula pendula*, are light and airy trees, casting dappled shade, and they are quick growing so do not take too long to provide the desired effect. There are other birches with whiter bark than *B.*

Fig. 8. *A small grotto, designed as part of a rock garden built into a bank. With water dripping from the roof into the pool, and plantings of ferns, this is indeed a cool, restful feature.*

pendula which you also might like to consider, such as *B. ermanii*, *B. jacque-montii*, *B. papyrifera* and *B. platyphylla szechuanica*, the latter very vigorous.

When planting a woodland area with other plants bear in mind there are two styles: the English woodland and the exotic woodland. You should choose one style and stick to it.

ENGLISH WOODLAND

The English woodland typically has carpets of bluebells (*Endymion nonscriptus*), primroses (*Primula vulgaris*) and windflowers (*Anemone nemorosa*) with white starry flowers. At the edge of the woodland plant bold drifts of daffodils, ideally the wild daffodil or lent lily, *Narcissus pseudonarcissus*, with pale yellow trumpets and white petals. These are all spring-flowering subjects, so as you can see an English woodland is at its most colourful in the spring.

Also found in English woodlands are shrubs such as holly (*Ilex aquifolium*), yew (*Taxus baccata*) and the spurge laurel, *Daphne laureola*, with attractive evergreen foliage and greenish yellow flowers in early spring.

Wild foxgloves (*Digitalis purpurea*) will provide colour in early summer with their spikes of purplish flowers. For winter colour the European stinking hellebore, *Helleborus foetidus*, would not look out of place with its yellow-green flowers above handsome evergreen foliage. It is a rare British native. A marvellous effect can be achieved by drifting snowdrops (*Galanthus nivalis*) around a group of hellebores.

EXOTIC WOODLAND

An exotic woodland is not quite so subtle as an English woodland – indeed, it is often a mass of bright colour. An exotic woodland is really only possible on an acid or lime-free soil, for most of the plants are lime haters.

This style of woodland is generally at its most colourful in spring and early summer, the colour being provided by rhododendrons, azaleas, camellias and magnolias.

There is a huge range of rhododendrons to choose from, including the hardy hybrids which will survive the coldest areas of the country. Popular ones include 'Britannia', crimson-scarlet; 'Christmas Cheer', white, early flowering; 'Cynthia', rose-crimson; 'Fastuosum Flore Pleno', deep mauve; 'Gomer Waterer', white, tinted mauve; 'Mrs G.W. Leak', pink, mottled with crimson; 'Pink Pearl', lilac-pink; and 'Purple Splendour', rich purple.

There are many species of rhododendron including *R. augustinii* with a profusion of blue flowers in spring. The violet-blue variety 'Electra' is even more eye-catching. Then there are spectacular large-leaved rhododendrons, such as *R. fictolacteum*, which need very sheltered conditions if they are to survive. The undersides of the leaves of this species are covered with bright brown 'felt' and large clusters of creamy white bell-shaped flowers are produced in late spring. The rhododendron with the largest leaves is *R. sinogrande*. They can grown to over 45 cm (18 in) in length, the upper surfaces being shiny while the undersides are covered with silvery 'felt'. It will not flower until it is semi-mature when it bears massive trusses of cream blooms, each with an eye-catching crimson blotch.

Riotous colour can be provided by azaleas in spring or early summer. There are deciduous kinds such as the Ghent, Knap Hill and Mollis hybrids, usually with trumpet-shaped flowers in a wide colour range; and the dwarf evergreen kinds like the famous Kurume hybrids.

Camellias provide colour in winter and spring, including the hundreds of varieties of *Camellia japonica*. Grow some *C. × williamsii* varieties, too, especially the popular 'Donation' with huge semi-double orchid-pink flowers.

Other shrubs for the exotic woodland include *Enkianthus campanulatus* with yellowy bronze cup-shaped flowers in spring; and the pieris with white lily-of-the-valley-like flowers in spring. Some pieris have brilliant red young foliage, such as *P.* 'Forest Flame' and *P. formosa forrestii* 'Wakehurst'. Among the best for flowers is *P. japonica* 'Purity' with clusters of pure white blooms.

Magnolias also have a place in the exotic woodland. There are many to choose from such as *M. × soulangiana* with goblet-shaped white flowers flushed with purple, and *M. stellata*, a medium-sized shrub with white starry flowers in spring.

Winter colour can be provided by witch hazels or hamamelis, such as the pale yellow *H. mollis* 'Pallida', or the coppery red *H. × intermedia*

A tranquil sitting area where one can while away the day amid luxuriant foliage plants and enjoy the fish in the garden pool.

'Jelena'. Try, too, the autumn cherry, *Prunus subhirtella* 'Autumnalis', a small tree bearing semi-double white flowers over the period mid-autumn to early spring.

For autumn colour there is nothing to beat the Japanese maples, varieties of *Acer palmatum*, which grow best in sheltered conditions. The lobed leaves of these large shrubs turn to brilliant shades of orange and red before they fall.

Among and around all of these shrubs plant drifts of suitable perennial plants, like the blue poppy, *Meconopsis betonicifolia*; and summer-flowering lilies such as the mid-century hybrids like orange 'Enchantment' and lemon yellow 'Destiny'. Make sure lilies receive plenty of sun, though.

The summer-flowering candelabra primulas will enjoy the dappled shade of the woodland and they like a cool moist soil. There are many to choose from including *P. bulleyana*, pale orange; *P. beesiana*, lilac-purple; and

P. *pulverulenta*, crimson. Then there is the drumstick primrose, *P. denticulata*, for spring colour. It has large globe-shaped heads of flowers which vary in colour from pale lilac to deep purple, rose and carmine. There is also a form, 'Alba', with white flowers.

To ensure shelter from cold winds for any rhododendrons and other shrubs which need it, plant the boundaries of the woodland with tough shrubs which will act as low-level windbreaks. A good choice includes the purple-flowered *Rhododendron ponticum* and the cherry laurel, *Prunus laurocerasus*, with glossy evergreen leaves and white flowers in spring, which is tolerant of shade.

The soil for all of the plants recommended needs to be moisture retentive and rich in humus, so add plenty of peat or leafmould before planting and mulch the plants with these materials. Finally, remember that the soil must be acid or lime-free.

This has all the elements of a secret garden — tall yew hedges with arches in them which provide tantalizing glimpses of this garden of annuals, when viewed from outside. Statuary act as focal points.

A FORMAL ROSE GARDEN

This is a group of geometrical beds with paths between them, in which are grown bush roses—large-flowered (hybrid teas) and/or cluster-flowered (floribundas). Formal rose gardens really became popular in the nineteenth century but it is interesting to note that the Romans had gardens devoted purely to roses and so did gardeners in medieval times, but in the past different kinds of roses were used (large-flowered and cluster-flowered were non-existent).

I suppose most people today would say that a garden devoted entirely to roses is impractical—indeed, due to lack of space in many gardens the trend is to grow roses with other plants.

However if you have the space and want a formal feature of some kind then a garden purely of roses is charming. It would be a good choice for a sunken garden where the soil is likely to remain moist, which is a basic requirement of successful rose growing. However, a rose garden can be sited anywhere, provided it receives full sun (another basic requirement).

The beds can be any shape desired—square, rectangular, circular, triangular, etc. You could have gravel paths between and around them—the blooms would show up well against this neutral background.

The best effect is achieved if only one variety of rose is planted in each bed. If you have, say, a group of five beds then plant a tall variety in the centre bed and plant roses of medium height in the surrounding beds. A standard rose planted in each bed will give variation in height and colour on a higher level. Ideally the standards should be the same varieties (or at least the same colours) as the bush roses.

A formal rose garden is traditionally surrounded by formal hedges such as yew or holly. Both are slow growing so it will take years for the desired effect to be achieved. You may prefer a faster-growing subject, such as Lawson cypress, but do choose a hedging plant with deep green foliage as this makes a marvellous background for roses. Do make sure the hedges are far enough away from the beds to prevent shadows across the roses, which must not be subjected to too much shade.

There are hundreds of varieties of large-flowered and cluster-flowered roses to choose from, but I would opt for highly fragrant varieties, as one of the delights of a rose garden is the scent on a warm summer's day.

AN OLD-FASHIONED HERB GARDEN

This is another rather extravagant feature where scents can be savoured on a summer's day. A traditional herb garden consists of a number of formal beds arranged in a geometrical pattern, with paths between them.

Herb gardens have been popular since medieval times. During that period mainly medicinal and culinary herbs were grown; today most people would want to grow more decorative kinds, but including some for the kitchen.

You should choose the sunniest part of your plot for a herb garden and ensure the soil is very well drained. The paths can be of gravel, natural stone paving or artificial paving slabs. The beds could be edged with low hedges of santolina or cotton lavender, with silvery evergreen aromatic foliage. The herb garden itself can be enclosed with formal hedges; perhaps of the sweet bay, *Laurus nobilis*, itself a culinary herb, if your garden is in a mild part of the country, otherwise with holly, yew etc.

Choice of herbs

There is a vast range of herbs to choose from. Popular culinary kinds include angelica, balm, basil, borage, caraway, chervil, chives, coriander, dill, fennel (also a highly ornamental plant), lovage, a wide range of mints (spearmint is probably the most useful), marjorams, parsley, rosemary (also quite an ornamental plant), savory, sage (very attractive are the purple and variegated varieties), tarragon and thymes.

Bergamot or *Monarda didyma* is most attractive with pink or red flowers in summer and is a herb of historical interest, as are chamomile with white daisy flowers in summer, rue which has beautiful glaucous foliage and southernwood with highly aromatic greyish green leaves. Other highly aromatic herbs include lavender, lemon verbena and myrtle.

——— A COURTYARD GARDEN ———

A courtyard is a cool, sheltered, intimate retreat which in warm climates is used to gain relief from the hot sun. In temperate climates, though, it has for long been favoured as a peaceful place to sit and relax. A true courtyard, as was built by the ancient Greeks and Romans, is surrounded completely by the house, with all the rooms leading into it, and open to the sky. A courtyard, though, does not really need to be completely enclosed – it can have walls on two or three sides only.

You could perhaps create a courtyard if you have high brick boundary walls – add another wall or two to enclose an area.

A courtyard garden should be simple. The Greeks and Romans furnished their courtyards with trees in containers and with statues. We could copy them, and also have a formal pool with a fountain. Complete the scene with a table and chairs and you have a quiet restful retreat.

Courtyards in Mediterranean countries are often paved with marble slabs. They are expensive in Britain, though, so you may prefer to lay pre-cast concrete paving slabs. I can recommend black and white slabs laid in a chequer-board pattern; or you could use pale grey and dark grey slabs.

The pool and fountain create a cool atmosphere and the restful sound of moving water. The pool itself should be of formal design, such as square or circular. Ideally it should be raised, built up with bricks. Place coping stones on top of the pool walls on which to sit and enjoy the fish.

Choose an attractive stone fountain for the centre of the pool – it can be as elaborate as you like. I particularly like tiered stone fountains where the water cascades from one bowl to another before reaching the pool.

Choice of plants

Choose some urns, vases and other ornamental containers in classical designs and plant them with large-leaved foliage plants such as *Fatsia japonica*, an evergreen shrub; the hardy palm, *Trachycarpus fortunei*; and plantain lilies or hostas. These can all be grown in partial shade.

Other plants I can recommend for a courtyard garden, but which need more sun, include trained grape vines, figs and citrus fruits. The latter

A sundial is a popular object for use as a focal point in a garden, here positioned at the end of a path, where one comes across a delightful planting of clematis and roses.

are not hardy and would have to be taken into a heated greenhouse or conservatory for the winter.

Hardy ferns would revel in cool shady corners while the arum lily, *Zantedeschia aethiopica*, would be happy in partial shade. It has bold white flowers and deep green arrow-shaped leaves.

The walls, of course, provide ideal supports for climbers. If the walls are shady grow subjects like ivies (particularly large-leaved variegated kinds), summer jasmine (*Jasminum officinale*) and the climbing hydrangea (*Hydrangea petiolaris*), the last two having white flowers. If a wall receives plenty of sun grow on it such plants as the blue passion flower (*Passiflora caerulea*) and grape vines.

INTIMATE SITTING AREAS

Most people like somewhere pleasant to sit in the garden, perhaps a sunny spot which is well secluded to create a quiet intimate atmosphere, and from the practical point of view to ensure shelter from the wind.

If your garden is well divided there should be no shortage of suitable areas which can be turned into peaceful and colourful little havens to while away the time.

SECLUDED SEAT

The area can be as simple as a seat partially surrounded by groups of flowering shrubs or a hedge. If the site has been put down to lawn it is a good idea to lay an area of paving for the seat, not only to prevent the grass becoming worn through constant use (nothing looks worse than bare, muddy patches in a lawn) but also to ensure dry conditions underfoot (paving dries out much faster than grass after a shower of rain).

This ornate fountain and pool are a major feature of this intimate courtyard garden which is made highly colourful in summer with plantings of impatiens or busy lizzie.

A SUMMERHOUSE

If you want to provide shelter from the elements why not consider a summerhouse? This can be an attractive feature in itself. For instance, some are made from western red cedar, an excellent choice for natural surroundings. There are several suppliers of summerhouses in Britain and models can be seen at show sites which are often attached to garden centres. Modern summerhouses are usually very simple, consisting of a single 'room' with windows. You may be lucky enough to find a rotating summerhouse which can be moved round to follow the sun.

The summerhouse is not a new idea, by any means, as it provided a retreat from the dwelling house as far back as the fifteenth century. Many styles have been seen over the centuries: Gothic, rustic, oriental etc.

There should, of course, be a pleasant view from the summerhouse, such as a pool or some other water feature, a rock garden, a colourful bed of summer bedding plants or a rose garden. An area in front of the summerhouse should be paved to provide a dry surface—you may want to sit outside during really fine weather. Alternatively consider timber decking which goes well with a timber summerhouse.

A summerhouse can also be used as a focal point in a garden. In this case there will be a long and hopefully pleasant view from the building.

A GAZEBO

Another idea is a gazebo, a garden building used as a vantage point, from which one can look out over an attractive part of the garden. A gazebo can have a seat in it and it should be partially screened. Such a structure can, like a summerhouse, be used as a focal point if desired.

The word gazebo was first recorded in 1752, so once again the idea is far from new. Modern gazebos are really like small open summerhouses, perhaps with a roof. A circular domed gazebo in wrought iron, painted white, makes a superb feature and an ideal support for climbing plants.

The DIY enthusiast could perhaps make a simple square timber gazebo, complete with roof.

A gazebo can be draped with summer-flowering climbers, especially scented ones, including the white-flowered jasmine, *Jasminum officinale*; honeysuckles like the early Dutch, *Lonicera periclymenum* 'Belgica', and the late Dutch, *L. p.* 'Serotina', both with yellowish and purplish flowers; wisteria, such as the lilac *W. floribunda* 'Macrobotrys'; and of course with climbing roses, some especially good scented ones being 'Compassion', salmon shaded orange; and 'Schoolgirl', coppery apricot flushed with pink.

AN ARBOUR

The dictionary definition of this feature is a bower or shady recess, natural or man-made. A natural shady recess could be formed with shrubs.

It would be quite easy to make an artificial arbour to partially enclose and cover a seat. A box-shaped structure could be made from trellis panels, open only at the front. Over this framework scented climbing plants could be grown—several examples have been described above. Alternatively you may like to train a grape vine over your arbour. One that I can particularly recommend is *Vitis vinifera* 'Brandt'. This is an ornamental vine, although the purple-black grapes can be eaten or made into wine. In the autumn the leaves take on colourful tints before they fall.

Once again, an arbour is far from a new idea—it was made as early as the Middle Ages. Try this feature—it is not often seen in gardens today and would be quite a novelty with your visitors. Don't forget to pave the 'floor' of your arbour to keep it dry underfoot.

Scented plants

Finally, remember that scented plants help to create atmosphere around any sitting area. As well as climbers, already mentioned, you could include shrubs and other plants which give off scent, such as the mock oranges or philadelphus, lilacs or syringas, and the common sweet briar, *Rosa eglanteria*, whose foliage is apple-scented, which is particularly pronounced after a shower of rain. This rose has small light pink blooms during the summer followed in autumn by heavy crops of hips. It grows to a height of about 1.8 m so could be included in a group of shrubs used to screen a sitting area.

Then there are many plants whose foliage has to be pinched to release the scent. These could be grouped close by a seat so that you can savour them as you sit. Try such kinds as lavender; the lemon-scented verbena, *Lippia citriodora*, slightly on the tender side; the common myrtle, *Myrtus communis*, also recommended only for mild areas; the lemon balm, *Melissa officinalis*; and even mints like *Mentha rotundifolia* or apple mint, and *M.* × *gentilis* 'Variegata' whose aromatic leaves are brightly splashed with yellow.

THE PATIO

The patio is a feature of many gardens today and it can make an intimate sitting area if partially enclosed. These days many people also use part of a patio as a barbecue area—there is a definite trend towards outdoor living and *al fresco* meals cooked on a barbecue are a welcome change from ordinary, everyday living.

We do not often use the term patio correctly today, for the true meaning is an inner courtyard of a house. What we mean today is a paved or some other form of hard area for sitting and general outdoor living. Often the patio is positioned near to the house (although it need not be) and in the sunniest part of the garden.

Certainly shelter from winds is desirable and this can be achieved by partially surrounding the patio with screens about 1.8 m (6 ft) high. Very popular is screen-block walling. Alternatively trellis screens could be erected. Both make ideal supports for climbing plants, choosing mainly fragrant summer-flowering kinds, for a patio is generally used only in good weather. Fencing panels could also be used to partially surround a patio, but for some people these may be too solid, creating a shut-in feeling.

Do be adventurous regarding the shape of the patio—far too many are simply square or rectangular, not very imaginative. A patio can be very irregular if desired, or it can be round, octagonal or some other geometric shape.

Surfacing materials

There are lots of materials to choose from for surfacing your patio. Probably pre-cast concrete paving slabs are most popular and a good choice for modern gardens. There is a range of sizes and shapes, including square, rectangular and hexagonal. The surfaces are often textured, some resembling natural stone. I would strongly advise, though, that you choose a non-slip surface. Slabs are available in natural stone colours, which are probably best for most gardens. Coloured slabs (green, pinks etc) could be a bit difficult to live with!

Natural-stone paving is more expensive but looks superb in any setting. It may be sandstone or limestone and can be bought as square slabs if you want a formal effect, or as random stone slabs for 'crazy paving', particularly appropriate for cottage and country gardens. Generally fairly wide gaps are left between random stone slabs, which are filled with soil and planted with creeping and carpeting plants such as thymes and raoulias.

A brick patio is a good choice for a cottage or country garden, or even for a contemporary setting if modern-looking bricks are chosen. You should use special hard paving bricks, or stock bricks for patios.

Various patterns can be created with bricks, such as herringbone, basketweave or a staggered effect, like bricks in a wall. They should be laid flat (not on edge), and loosely, with 9 mm ($\frac{3}{8}$ in) joints which are filled with sand.

Concrete should not be dismissed as a possible surface—I know that it can be hard work mixing it, though! The alternative is to have ready-mixed concrete delivered. It is a good choice for a modern setting. You can have a textured surface, achieved by lightly brushing the concrete while it is still wet to expose the aggregates. Concrete can also be coloured, with the aid of proprietary colouring powders. This avoids the problem of glare during bright sunny periods.

Gravel makes a good surface, provided you don't mind the crunching sound when you walk on it. Gravel is a good choice for both country and town gardens; it goes with any style of garden or architecture. Pea shingle is used to create a gravelled area, spread 2.5 cm (1 in) deep over well-rammed soil. The area needs to be edged with small curbing stones or bricks to prevent the gravel from spreading.

Timber decking is probably more popular in America than in Britain, although it is catching on in this country. It is an excellent choice for natural or country gardens. The decking is supported on stout timber posts but is raised only a few inches above the ground. Western red cedar is often used for decking, together with chestnut, deal and pine. All should be thoroughly treated with timber preservative, of course. Coloured preservatives are available, such as red cedar, dark oak and chestnut. Timber decking can be bought ready made, in sections, or you could make your own.

Materials can be mixed if desired to create interesting variations in texture, particularly if you want a large expanse of paving or concrete. For instance, you could have areas of cobbies, gravel or granite setts with paving slabs or concrete; or lay a brick edging around a paved patio, which gives a good contrast in colour and texture.

Low-growing plants in the patio also help to create an interesting surface, so ensure plenty of planting areas when laying a patio. For instance,

Opposite: This highly ornate fountain and pool in a cool shady courtyard is surrounded by foliage plants such as bamboos and ivies.

leave out paving slabs here and there to provide little beds for low-growing plants like thymes, raoulias, aubrietas, alyssum and alpine phloxes.

With the aid of wooden shuttering you can form similar beds in a concrete patio. Planting areas can be formed in gravel, too, by leaving the soil unfirmed here and there. After planting, the gravel can be laid around and among the plants.

Special features

Many people find the sound of moving water very relaxing, so a formal pool with a fountain could be incorporated into a patio. An attractive modern feature is a bubble fountain trickling over a millstone, or at least a concrete imitation. The water trickles down through shingle surrounding the stone, into a sump. It is circulated by means of a small electric pump.

Another feature that you may like to incorporate into a patio is a pergola, which could cover part of the area to provide shade. A pergola makes an excellent support for climbing plants – I particularly like to have a grape vine growing over it such as the ornamental *Vitis vinifera* 'Brandt'. A wisteria is a good choice, too. Both are very leafy climbers, so providing dappled shade. The pergola is a descendant of the fifteenth- and sixteenth-century covered walk (also known as an arbour), constructed of trellis or some other form of timber framework, with an arched top and supporting climbing plants.

Pergolas today have flat tops and can be any shape desired. They consist of a series of pillars supporting horizontal beams and cross-pieces. Modern timber pergola kits are available, in western red cedar, or they may be painted white. A rustic pergola would be more appropriate for a cottage or country garden.

A more substantial and permanent pergola has brick or stone pillars supporting the timber beams and cross-pieces. The height of the pillars is usually 2.4 m (8 ft) and they are spaced 1.8–2.4 m (6–8 ft) apart. Timber uprights must be sunk at least 60 cm (2 ft) into the ground and ideally concreted in.

Barbecues

Barbecues are popular today and often feature on modern patios. There are many purpose-made charcoal-fuelled portable barbecues available, both simple and sophisticated. Alternatively you may prefer to build your own permanent barbecue. It can be constructed of bricks, stone or ornamental concrete walling blocks to match the patio. Basically it is a box-shaped structure but with an open front and top. It can be built by first laying six courses of bricks to support the metal fire tray. Then four more courses are built on top and these support the metal grill (a metal shoe scraper makes a good grill). Three more courses of bricks can be laid above the grill to act as a wind shield. Brick cupboards could be built alongside the barbecue for the storage of charcoal, utensils etc, not forgetting a flat working surface for food preparation and serving.

Ornamental containers

Ornamental containers could be dotted around the patio and planted with colourful plants. There are many types including traditional terracotta clay

Fig. 9. Opposite: *A rather grand feature, but nevertheless in keeping in a large garden of a period house – a terrace, complete with stone balustrade, looking down onto a parterre, planted with colourful bedding plants (see p.66).*

pots, both plain English-style pots and fancy Venetian, Tuscan, Florentine and Minoan styles. Glazed terracotta is also available. Large pots are ideal for colourful spring and summer bedding plants like pelargoniums, French marigolds and begonias.

Narrow-necked urns and jars are attractive even without plants in them. They are in the style of ancient Roman and Greek funerary urns and have been popular since the seventeenth century for garden decoration. They are not too easy to plant due to their narrow necks and many plants look out of proportion to the containers. However, try growing trailing plants in them, such as ivy-leaved pelargoniums and petunias for summer colour. If space allows set a taller plant in the centre such as a small specimen of the cabbage palm, *Cordyline australis.*

In a very modern setting low flat concrete bowls can be filled with colourful summer and spring bedding plants. These have been popular since the 1950s: they made an appearance at the Festival of Britain (I seem to remember!).

Wooden tubs are a good choice for patios in cottage and country gardens, filled perhaps with old-fashioned flowers such as nicotiana (ornamental tobacco) and antirrhinums. For modern settings there is a wide range of concrete tubs available, while imitation-stone tubs look good in an informal setting.

This secluded seat is in an arbour formed by scented shrubs such as philadelphus or mock orange. The golden robinia provides foliage colour throughout the summer.

A very secret seat surrounded by plantings of lime-green Alchemilla mollis, *or lady's mantle, and white astilbes — a very soothing atmosphere.*

WATER GARDENS

Water gardens are certainly romantic features, whether for purely decorative effect, primarily for growing aquatic plants, or both. They have been garden features for thousands of years. It is known that the Ancient Egyptians grew aquatics like waterlilies and papyrus.

In Europe water gardens were formal features from Roman times until the eighteenth century, the advent of aquatic-plant cultivation. The growing of water plants became extremely popular in the nineteenth century and is still enjoyed by countless gardeners today.

Water can be either still or moving, but one should bear in mind that moving water is not suitable for some aquatic plants, particularly waterlilies. Moving water, though, gives a new dimension to a garden and its sound can be very relaxing.

A reasonably large expanse of still water has the attraction of reflections from plants and clouds.

A water garden or feature is certainly recommended as an idea for a secret garden but bear in mind that it should be sited in a spot which receives full sun; and it should not be overhung by trees, shrubs etc, which can shade the water and whose leaves falling into the water will pollute it.

A water feature can make an excellent focal point in a garden, to draw the eye. A large expanse of water can be recommended as a feature that can be seen from a summerhouse, gazebo or other sitting area.

The type of water feature chosen should of course suit the style of garden. One has a choice of a formal or informal feature. The most popular type of water feature today is undoubtedly the garden pool.

A FORMAL POOL

A formal pool may be circular, square or rectangular. It would make a nice feature in a patio area or courtyard, in a formal rose or sunken garden, or it could be used as a focal point (especially if equipped with a fountain), in a suitable part of the garden. A pool can be at ground level or it can be raised, the sides being built up with bricks or concrete walling blocks. Pool construction is easy today with the use of pool liners in such materials as butyl rubber and PVC. There is more about construction in Chapter 6.

Fountains have for long been features of formal water gardens: they were used by the Romans, and the idea was developed in Renaissance Italy and then spread all over Europe. Fountains in large gardens and estates were often highly complex.

A simple fountain is easily achieved today with a complete kit, consisting of the fountain unit and a submersible electric pump (see Chapter 6). The bubbler or bubble fountain is a comparatively modern idea and is generally used as a feature in its own right (see patios, in this chapter).

THE CANAL

Another formal water feature is the canal, which is a long, narrow, straight stretch of water. It was once a popular feature in formal gardens and often had a fountain incorporated. The canal is not much used today, although in my opinion it would make a good feature in a formal garden; it could be used to carry the eye to a piece of sculpture or a fountain at the far end.

INFORMAL POOL

In a natural setting an informal, irregular-shaped water feature is recommended. Again this is very easy to achieve with the aid of a flexible pool liner. A natural-looking pool should, of course, be at ground level (in other words, not raised above it). A large informal pool could have a row of stepping stones across it.

If you want moving water do not opt for a fountain, which is not appropriate for an informal pool. Instead go for a waterfall or cascade, ideally coursing through a rock garden into a pool below. Try to make a waterfall as natural-looking as possible, forming it with rocks rather like a flight of steps. Details of how to build a waterfall will be found in Chapter 6.

A STREAM

A stream is a delightful feature in a natural garden and its banks could be planted with moisture-loving or bog plants. Some gardeners are fortunate enough to have a natural stream running through the garden, but once again an artificial stream is easily made by lining the excavation with flexible pool liner. A stream should, of course, have a beginning and an end, and perhaps this is best achieved by using it to link together two pools, positioned some distance apart. Make the stream winding—not straight like a canal. A stream could be used to link one secret garden with another.

BOG GARDEN

An area of wet soil for bog or marsh plants is another feature that could be incorporated into the informal water garden. Usually a bog garden is positioned immediately adjacent to the pool so that overflowing water keeps the soil very moist.

CHOICE OF WATER AND BOG PLANTS

A selection of popular aquatic and moisture-loving plants is as follows:

Waterlilies

Botanically known as *Nymphaea*, the waterlilies are the most popular aquatics for pools, but bear in mind they dislike moving water.

They range from miniature kinds for water no more than 15 cm (6 in) deep, like white-flowered *N. pygmaea* 'Alba' and yellow *N. pygmaea* 'Helvola', to large kinds for 90 cm (3 ft) of water, like the *marliacea* types. Popular is the yellow *N. marliacea* 'Chromatella', and pink 'Rosea' and 'Carnea'. In between are the *laydeckeri* waterlilies which are suitable for small pools with a depth of water around 30–45 cm (12–18 in), like red 'Purpurata', white 'Alba' and carmine 'Lilacea'.

Marginal aquatics

For the shallow water at the edge of pools marginal plants should be grouped, such as water irises—blue *I. laevigata* and yellow *I. pseudacorus*; the flowering rush, *Butomus umbellatus*, with heads of deep pink flowers; the arrowhead, *Sagittaria japonica*, with white flowers (double in the form 'Flore Pleno'); the double marsh marigold, *Caltha palustris* 'Flore Pleno', with golden yellow spring blooms; the water plantain, *Alisma plantago-aquatica*, with panicles of pink blooms; the bog arum, *Calla palustris*, with white spathes; and the pickerel weed, *Pontederia cordata*, with spikes of blue flowers.

Deep-water plants

For the middle of deep pools try the golden club, *Orontium aquaticum*, with spikes of golden flowers, and the water hawthorn, *Aponogeton distachyus*, with a long succession of white blooms.

Floating plants

Some aquatics float on the surface of pools, such as the water chestnut, *Trapa natans*, with rosettes of deep green leaves; the frogbit, *Hydrocharis morsus-ranae*, with rosettes of kidney-shaped leaves, ideal for small pools; and the water soldier, *Stratiotes aloides*, with bronzy green spiny foliage carried in a large rosette.

Submerged oxygenating plants

'Water weeds' help to ensure a well-balanced pool and supply the water with oxygen, particularly important if you keep fish. There are several kinds to choose from like the common fish weed, *Lagarosiphon major*; Canadian pondweed, *Elodea canadensis*; the water violet, *Hottonia palustris*; the water crowfoot, *Ranunculus aquatilis*; and the milfoils, species of *Myriophyllum*.

Bog plants

These plants need moist conditions but do not like to actually stand in water. Good examples are the hostas or plantain lilies, grown mainly for their bold foliage; irises like *I. kaempferi* and *I. sibirica*; astilbes with their handsome feathery plumes of flowers; the bog primulas like *P. rosea, P. aurantiaca, P. japonica, P. pulverulenta, P. bulleyana* and *P. florindae*. Globe flowers or trollius are superb bog plants for spring colour with their globe-shaped yellow or orange blooms.

A SCENTED GARDEN

This perhaps is rather an extravagant idea for a secret garden, grouping together lots of scented plants, but of course no problem if you have the space. Scents can come from flowers and leaves and for best results you should choose a very warm, sheltered spot. With most scented plants the warmer the conditions the more pronounced their scent. Scent is quickly dispersed by wind, so at all costs avoid a windy spot for a scented garden.

The centre of the garden could feature a chamomile lawn, which scents the air at every step. This first became fashionable in the seventeenth century. To make a chamomile lawn you will need the non-flowering variety called 'Treneague'. It is evergreen with deep green finely divided leaves, which are highly aromatic when crushed, and it grows to 2.5–5 cm (1–2 in) high. The creeping stems root into the soil as they spread. It will be happy in a dry sunny place, is suitable for light soils and will not tolerate shade.

A chamomile lawn is made by planting young plants in the spring, spacing them about 15 cm (6 in) apart each way. The lawn should be trimmed in late summer with a mower or shears to maintain a neat and tidy appearance.

There are lots of scented shrubs to plant in beds surrounding the chamomile lawn and many of the flowering kinds attract butterflies and bees. Some good scented shrubs are listed below.

Shrubs with scented flowers

Choisya ternata (Mexican orange blossom) Strong spicy orange-blossom scent.
Cytisus battandieri Has a strong fruity pineapple scent.
Daphne × burkwoodii Deliciously sweet scent.
Magnolia denudata A strong, rich sweet scent.
Osmanthus delavayi This has a strong, sweet heavy scent.
× *Osmarea burkwoodii* Similar to osmanthus.
Philadelphus × lemoinei (mock orange) Strong orange blossom scent.
Ribes odoratum (golden currant) Strong honey scent.

Part of a scented garden, with carpeting thymes growing in the paving and a white-flowered, aromatic chrysanthemum, superbly set off by a purple-leaved cotinus or smoke bush (garden designer: Michael Branch).

Skimmia japonica 'Fragrans'   Reminiscent of lily-of-the-valley.
Spartium junceum (Spanish broom)   Strong, sweet orangey scent.
Syringa vulgaris varieties (lilac)   Strong, sweet heady scent.
Ulex europaeus 'Plenus' (double gorse)   A strong, heady honey scent.
Viburnum carlesii   This has a strong, sweet carnation-like scent.

There are several winter-flowering shrubs with strongly scented flowers and I have described these under The Winter Garden (see below).

Shrubs with scented foliage
Most of these only release their scent if the foliage is pinched or crushed.
Cistus ladanifer (sun rose)   Strong resinous scent, freely given off in hot weather.

Eucalyptus gunnii (cider gum)   Fresh camphorous scent when leaves are crushed. Grow it as a shrub by hard pruning each year.

Laurus nobilis (sweet bay)   Strong aromatic camphorous scent when crushed.

Lavandula spica (lavender)   Strong distinctive scent when crushed. Flowers also scented.

Myrtus communis (common myrtle)   Strong aromatic scent when crushed.

Perovskia atriplicifolia   Strong camphorous scent when crushed.

Rosa eglanteria (common sweet briar)   Leaves give off strong apple scent after rain.

Rosmarinus officinalis (rosemary)   Strong, aromatic, spicy camphorous scent when crushed. Also freely gives off scent.

Santolina chamaecyparissus (cotton lavender)   Stong aromatic camphorous scent when crushed.

———— *THE WINTER GARDEN* ————

Like the scented garden, this can also be considered a rather extravagant idea but an appealing one if you have the space. Plants with winter interest are often dull at other times of year, so group them together in some secluded part of the garden and visit them frequently when they are at their best, and ignore them for the remainder of the year!

One can create some very attractive planting schemes using plants with winter interest. Some of the flowering kinds need a solid dark green background if the flowers are to show up well. This can be provided by the evergreen *Viburnum tinus*, or laurustinus, itself a winter-flowering shrub with a long succession of white flowers. *Garrya elliptica* also makes a good background and bears jade catkins in winter. A large garrya makes a marvellous host for the winter jasmine, *Jasminum nudiflorum*, with its bright yellow blooms.

Deep green hedges and groups of other evergreen shrubs can also be used as backgrounds for winter-flowering shrubs like *Chimonanthus praecox*, or winter sweet, with its sweetly scented waxy pale yellow flowers; the shrubby honeysuckles, *Lonicera fragrantissima* and *L.* × *purpusii*, with sweetly scented cream flowers; *Daphne mezereum*, with sweetly scented purple-red flowers; and the delightfully scented viburnums like *V.* × *bodnantense* 'Dawn', palest pink, and *V. farreri*, white.

The winter-flowering cherry, *Prunus subhirtella* 'Autumnalis', with small semi-double white flowers, and the blush pink 'Autumnalis Rosea', certainly need a solid dark background. As they are small trees something quite tall will be needed, such as a group of large conifers.

The witch hazels, too, eventually make large shrubs. There is a good selection including *Hamamelis mollis* 'Pallida' and 'Goldcrest' with yellow flowers, and *H.* × *intermedia* 'Diane' and 'Jelena' with coppery red flowers.

Among these deciduous shrubs and trees should be planted some evergreens like the winter-flowering *Mahonia japonica* with large dramatic leaves and huge racemes of yellow flowers scented like lily-of-the-valley; and *Daphne odora* whose purple-pink flowers have a rich sweet scent. Valued for its bright gold-splashed foliage is *Elaeagnus pungens* 'Maculata'.

Shrubs with coloured bark are also highly recommended for the winter garden, particularly *Cornus alba* 'Sibirica', the Westonbirt dogwood, with brilliant crimson stems, and the yellow-stemmed *C. stolonifera* 'Flaviramea'. These are best planted in bold groups and look superb with *Mahonia japonica* or *Viburnum tinus*.

The cornus should be cut back almost to the ground in early spring each year to encourage thickets of young stems which have the brightest colour. The same treatment should be given to the scarlet willow, *Salix alba* 'Chermesina', whose young stems are brilliant orange-scarlet. The white-washed brambles, *Rubus cockburnianus* and *R. thibetanus*, should also be pruned hard. The young stems are covered in a white bloom, which contrast marvellously with dark evergreen shrubs and with the cornus and willow.

Prunus serrula is a small tree with reddish brown shiny bark which shows up well in winter. Small white flowers appear in mid-spring.

Winter-flowering heathers can be planted in bold drifts at the front of these shrubs, or around the trees. There are many varieties of *Erica herbacea (E. carnea)* like the ever-popular 'Springwood Pink' and 'Springwood White'. Don't forget some golden-foliage varieties, too, like *E.h.* 'Ann Sparkes' and 'Foxhollow'. Varieties of *E. × darleyensis* flower throughout winter. One of my favourites is 'Silberschmelze' ('Molten Silver') with a profusion of white flowers—try planting a drift around *Prunus serrula* for contrast in colour and texture.

Groups of snowdrops, *Galanthus nivalis*, will complete the scene in the winter garden: they can be planted around the shrubs and even allowed to grow through carpets of winter-flowering heathers.

THE GARDEN ROOM OR CONSERVATORY

In this secret garden exotic flowers and foliage can be enjoyed all the year round. There is great interest in conservatories today—many people are investing in them not only to provide extra living space but also to grow and display exotic plants.

A conservatory is an integral part of the house, with access from a room, such as a lounge or dining room, and makes a pleasant peaceful retreat for a quiet drink after dinner!

Conservatories, particularly for entertaining, have been popular for several centuries and were certainly all the rage with the Victorians, when they were considered an essential part of the social structure. The conservatory's main role then was for entertaining amid luxuriant plant growth.

From the nineteenth century many shapes of conservatory were built, such as dome-shaped, half-dome, curvilinear, hexagonal and octagonal.

Victorian-style conservatories are very popular today, together with Georgian and Gothic styles. There are, too, many modern designs. It is best to choose a conservatory which suits the style of your house. Very popular are the modular conservatories, which are designed for the customer's requirements. The manufacturers produce standardized units or modules and these can be fitted together in an infinite variety of designs. The customer gets the equivalent of a custom-built conservatory for a realistic price.

White flowers and silver and green foliage plants help to create a retreat with a 'cool' atmosphere. A statue very much enhances this planting.

Of course, modular conservatories are not cheap, but there are many modestly priced conservatories available in the form of mass-produced self-assembly kits.

Modern conservatories are made either from timber (usually western red cedar) or aluminium alloy. Again it is sensible to choose a material which suits the style of your house. Many conservatories are built on low walls of brick or timber, but it is possible to obtain designs with glass to ground level. A conservatory should ideally be sited where it receives as much sun as possible, such as a south- or west-facing wall, and it should be sheltered from the wind, for cold winds can result in rapid heat loss, which means higher heating bills.

Remember that it is essential to liaise with your local planning authority when you are intending to build a conservatory.

A good way to link the conservatory with the rest of the garden is to build a patio around it, which can be used as a sitting area and for displaying colourful plants in containers.

Choosing plants

The kinds of plants you will be able to grow in the conservatory will depend on the temperature you are able to provide. With a steady temperature of between 15 and 21°C (60–70°F), which provides an ideal atmosphere for living in, too, you can grow tropical and sub-tropical flowering and foliage plants: exotic climbers like allamanda, bougainvillea and stephanotis; shrubs such as oleander (nerium), gardenia, tibouchina and crossandra; and flowering and foliage pot plants, including anthurium, begonias, saint-paulias, codiaeums, monsteras, palms, philodendrons, cordylines, dracaenas, and rubber plants and figs (ficus).

Of course, such warm conditions are not cheap to maintain, so many people opt for an 'intermediate' conservatory, with a minimum winter temperature of 10°C (50°F), or a 'cool' conservatory, with a minimum winter temperature of 4.5 to 7°C (40 to 45°F). There are many plants that can be grown in these conditions, including a wide range of the most popular pot plants, such as calceolarias, primulas, cinerarias, fuchsias, pelargoniums, streptocarpus and cyclamen. Various climbers, too, would thrive, like bougainvillea, hoya, lapageria, passiflora and plumbago. And don't forget fruits such as citrus, a grape vine, peaches and figs.

Water gardens are certainly romantic features and may be purely for decorative effect, for growing plants, or both. Here, arum lilies or zantedeschias are featured.

Other features

You can have various features in a conservatory, even a small pool if desired. Statuary can provide atmosphere, and large plants can be grown in ornamental containers, such as wooden tubs in traditional styles.

The conservatory should be comfortably furnished with chairs and table. There is a wide range appropriate for use in a conservatory. For instance, tables and chairs can be obtained in cast aluminium, intricately patterned, resembling the cast-iron furniture of times past. Usually they are painted white. Alternatively you may prefer timber table and chairs: the kinds designed for garden use look good in a conservatory. I am particularly fond of cane furniture: it seems a natural choice for a conservatory as it associates well with plants. There is a very wide choice of tubular aluminium furniture and this looks particularly attractive in a modern setting. It is available plastic-coated. Then there is a big range of upholstered garden or conservatory chairs if you want a bit more comfort when relaxing.

—— A CHILDREN'S PLAY AREA ——

In the context of romantic secret gardens a children's play area should stimulate a sense of adventure. I am thinking of a secret play area for older children—those who no longer require constant parental supervision. I am certainly not advocating a secret area for very tiny children, whose play area should be near the house where it can be easily seen.

The area should be well enclosed with a strong screen of some kind. A screen of tough, tall evergreen shrubs, perhaps; or for instant effect a 1.8 m (6 ft) high palisade of logs.

There could be some form of shelter, for play in wet weather. This can be as simple as a wooden framework supporting a tarpaulin. Alternatively it could be a log cabin or even an old garden shed. A tree house can be exciting for children, with access by a rope ladder. Tree houses used to be popular in many countries, with adults as well as children, but today they are largely neglected. If you do not have a suitable large tree then consider building a small house or cabin on stilts to raise it well above ground.

Jungle-like conditions are guaranteed to stimulate children's imagination so how about an area of densely planted tall tough shrubs? Include some clumps of bamboo, too. Of course, such a feature takes time to establish so you will have to plant it while your children are still tiny, so that it's ready for them as they become older.

Out of all the play equipment for children perhaps the climbing frame will prove most exciting, especially if it is well equipped with rope-ladders, lengths of rope, etc. By all means have a see-saw, slide and swing if your children want these.

A pet's corner is ideally sited in such a play area. It's a nice idea to have wire-netting runs for such pets as rabbits and guinea pigs as well as the normal hutches. It's good to see pets roaming around in a large but secure grassy area. They should not be left unattended in open-topped runs, though, for fear of foxes and cats getting at them.

You should carefully consider suitable surfaces for children to play on. Perhaps most of the play area can be left natural as it will take a lot of punish-

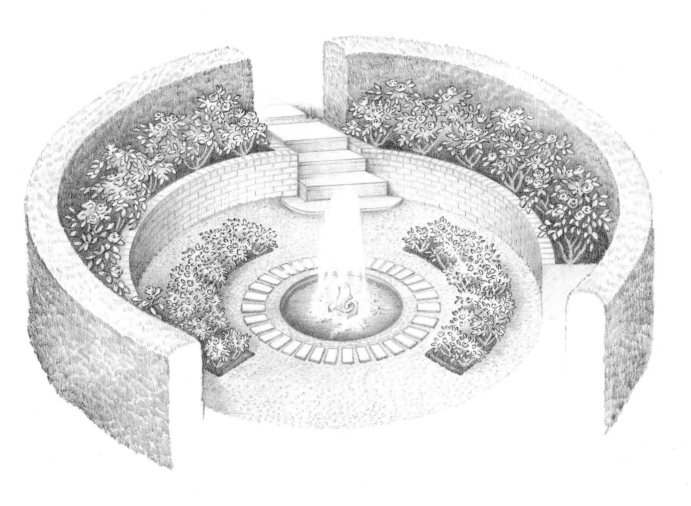

ment. Grass, for instance, may not last long. The area containing play equipment like climbing frames, see-saw, slide and swing should be surfaced with soft material. Ideal for this is pulverized or shredded bark which can be bought in bags from garden centres. It stops the area from becoming muddy, too. A harder area for play, as in front of a log cabin or other play house, could be provided by timber decking. This gives a comparatively dry, mud-free area in wet weather.

Fig. 10. The normal shape of a sunken garden is square or rectangular, so this circular design is very unusual. The garden is screened with a hedge and planted with roses. A pool with a fountain makes an attractive central feature.

THE TERRACE

A terrace is a raised flat area surrounded with a stone balustrade, although the word is misused today to mean any flat paved sitting area. A feature of gardens since the Roman and Ancient Egyptian periods, the terrace is normally built adjacent to the house with access from one of the rooms and is used for sitting and entertaining.

If the garden naturally falls away from your house you have a good site for a terrace, which can be built up with brick or stone walls and paved with pre-cast concrete slabs. Ready-made balustrade can be bought (usually in simulated stone).

Immediately below a terrace you may have an ideal site for a parterre, a feature which should be viewed from above—see Fig. 9. Parterre is a French word, meaning a level area of ornamental flower beds, and it first became known in Britain in the seventeenth century. The parterre was usually a rectangular area containing many small beds forming intricate patterns, the area often being surrounded by formal hedges or stone balustrades. The Italians and the French were noted for developing the parterre in the sixteenth century. The beds contained dwarf, sometimes colourful, plants and were surrounded by paths.

Both the terrace and the parterre are out of fashion today, but my aim is to bring romance back into gardening, so why not consider them as a combined feature in your garden? Fig. 9 shows a relatively simple arrangement of beds. The surrounds and paths could be of gravel and the beds edged with the edging box, *Buxus sempervirens* 'Suffruticosa'. It is used as a low formal hedge. The beds could be filled with colourful bedding plants, both spring and summer kinds. There will, of course, be a lot of hedge clipping to do, but the job could be speeded up by using an electric hedge trimmer.

THE SUNKEN GARDEN

This is a garden sunk below ground level and is a good idea if you have a natural deep hollow in your garden. It has been a garden feature since the Tudor period and the usual shape is square or rectangular (formal in every aspect), but my design, Fig. 10, is more unusual as it is circular.

The depth of a sunken garden is usually about 60 cm (2 ft) and the walling can be of bricks or stone. Access is by means of steps.

The garden can be screened with a hedge, or with trellis which can support climbing plants. Set the screen far enough back from the sunken area to create a bed or border for planting. This is, in effect, a raised bed or border although it is the natural level of the surrounding garden.

As the soil may be naturally moister in a sunken garden it would be a good place to grow roses, as I have shown in my design. A pool with a fountain makes an attractive central feature.

Alternatively you could plant the beds with bedding plants, both spring and summer flowering kinds.

If the soil is very wet it would be a better idea to create a bog garden, using moisture-loving plants. You could have a pool, too, of course.

The sunken garden, then, is a very imaginative idea, but also very practical if you have a suitable site.

5
FURTHER IDEAS FOR SECRET GARDENS

These are ordinary, more down-to-earth ideas but nevertheless are attractive features, some being suitable for large gardens, others for medium-sized and small plots. Most of these ideas are modern, or comparatively modern, and are found in many private gardens today.

——— THE WALLED GARDEN ———

This is not one of the modern ideas, for the walled garden was once a feature of many large gardens and private estates. A walled garden is a large area completely enclosed by high walls, generally in the form of a square. Walled gardens are sheltered and any wall which receives full sun is a very warm

Statuary often needs a background of dark green foliage to show it to best advantage. Here dark green ivy makes the perfect backcloth.

place indeed. Hence, in the old days walled gardens were often used for growing vegetables and fruits for the house as the warm micro-climate favoured early crops. Often, vegetables and fruit bushes would be grown in the centre of the garden and trained fruit trees on the sunny walls. Sometimes a lean-to greenhouse would be included on one of the walls and used for growing such fruits as grapes and melons.

If you are lucky enough to possess a walled garden I suggest you would not do much better than devote it to fruits and vegetables. On the walls which receive full sun you could grow fan-trained peaches, nectarines, cherries and plums, and espalier apples and pears. You may like to grow a fig against one wall, bearing in mind, though, that it would take up a lot of space. You could certainly concentrate on early vegetables, starting them off under cloches for further protection.

I am not suggesting that you actually build a walled garden from scratch, as it would cost a small fortune! Rather that best use is made of an existing one. If you do not want to grow fruits on the walls then how about some attractive ornamental climbers and wall shrubs? There are some very choice kinds available and some of them are on the tender side, needing a really sheltered spot in full sun. No problem if you have a walled garden. Choose your sunniest walls for them. Let's take a look at some of these suitable plants.

Wall shrubs and climbers

There are some beautiful abutilons available today, including the well-known *A. megapotamicum* with red and yellow bell-shaped flowers in summer and autumn. One of the most spectacular in my opinion is *A. × suntense* 'Jermyns' with masses of large saucer-shaped deep mauve flowers in summer, set against greyish foliage.

Carpenteria californica is a superb evergreen wall shrub which, in midsummer, produces large white flowers each with a boss of gold stamens. Many of the evergreen ceanothus of Californian lilacs are best grown on warm sunny walls, like *C. arboreus* 'Trewithen Blue', 'Burkwoodii', 'Cascade' and *C. impressus*. All have masses of blue flowers in spring or summer. The lobster's claw, *Clianthus puniceus*, is truly spectacular, with clusters of brilliant red claw-like flowers in early summer. It is a semi-evergreen with attractive pinnate leaves.

Desfontainea spinosa is an evergreen shrub with holly-like leaves and in late summer produces scarlet and yellow tubular flowers. It will not succeed in shallow chalky soils. *Fremontodendron californicum* (also known as *Fremontia*), and the hybrid 'California Glory', have large cup-shaped golden flowers in summer and are evergreen shrubs. The shrubby veronica, *Hebe hulkeana*, is quite tender and certainly needs a warm sheltered position. This small evergreen shrub flowers in late spring and early summer, producing panicles of flowers in pale lavender-blue.

Leptospermum scoparium and its varieties come from New Zealand and are on the tender side. These shrubs are evergreen, with masses of starry flowers in late spring and early summer in shades of red, pink and also white.

Also from New Zealand is *Sophora tetraptera* with clusters of deep yellow tubular flowers in spring. With large blooms is the variety 'Grandiflora'. These shrubs have deciduous pinnate leaves.

These are all classed as wall shrubs, which are grown against walls but not actually trained to them. Let us now consider some climbing plants, which will need some suitable supports such as horizontal wires or trellis panels fixed to the wall.

The trumpet vine, *Campsis radicans*, is truly spectacular with vivid orange and scarlet trumpet-shaped flowers in late summer and early autumn. It clings by means of aerial roots. There is a hybrid called *C. × tagliabuana* 'Madame Galen' with salmon-red flowers which is very vigorous.

The passion flowers would be ideal for a sheltered walled garden and need a wall in full sun. There's the blue passion flower, *Passiflora caerulea*, its white variety 'Constance Elliott', and *P. edulis*, the granadilla, with white, green and purple flowers. They bloom in the summer.

Tecomaria capensis is a vigorous, quite tender twining plant only suitable for the most sheltered spots in mild areas. It has pinnate foliage and vivid scarlet trumpet-shaped flowers in late summer. The self-clinging climber *Trachelospermum asiaticum* has highly fragrant cream starry flowers in summer. The deep green glossy foliage is evergreen.

THE WILDLIFE GARDEN

Interest in the conservation of wildlife has never been stronger than it is today. Many areas of land all over the country are being designated conservation sites, to preserve our wild flowers and fauna. And many private gardeners are devoting parts of their gardens to wildlife habitats. These are not necessarily large gardens, either. It is surprising what can be done even in a pocket-handkerchief plot. Indeed this is well demonstrated at the Chelsea Flower Show where small gardens, designed and planted to attract wildlife, have become a regular feature in recent years.

So I do urge you to devote one of your secret areas to a wildlife sanctuary; and if space permits, creating several different habitats.

A vast range of wild flowers can be raised from seeds, bought from a specialist supplier. You can either buy them as individual species, or as collections for different conditions and habitats: for instance, there are collections for chalk grassland, for a cornfield, a hedgerow, meadow, pond-edge, acid grassland and woodland edge.

For grassland habitats you can buy wild flower seeds mixed with grass seed. Alternatively you can establish a grass area first and then plant wild flowers in it. For instance, you can raise them from seeds and grow on the seedlings in pots, or you can buy young plants from a specialist supplier.

Let us take a look at the various wildlife habitats that it is possible to create. Bear in mind that these do not have to be large areas and even a small garden can contain several. They can either be all grouped together in one part of the garden, or spread around if preferred.

CORNFIELD

This is a popular habitat with many people for the wild flowers provide lots of colour in the summer and attract butterflies, bees and other insects. Cornfield flowers are annuals and ideal for poor soils. Typical cornfield annuals

A secluded area in early summer, with a carpet of lime-green Alchemilla mollis or lady's mantle, and scented white philadelphus or mock orange.

include mayweed, field poppy, corn marigold, heartsease, cornflower, charlock and corncockle. There's no need to grow them in grass—sow direct into prepared ground. They will flower in the summer and should then self-sow in successive years.

MINI-MEADOW

This is an area of grass which is allowed to grow long, containing wild flowers suited to soil type: for instance, harebells and bird's foot trefoil for acid soils; meadow buttercup, cowslips, yarrow, ox-eye daisy, self-heal and lady's smock for alkaline or chalky soils. A mini-meadow will attract butterflies (for instance, bird's foot trefoil encourages the common blue butterfly and the lady's smock the orange-tip and green-veined white), and other creatures like grasshoppers. A mini-meadow is a good choice for poor soil and it can be achieved either by sowing a grass seed/wild flower mixture, or by first establishing the grass area and then planting in it pot-grown plants, setting them in bold groups. Cut the grass to about 5 cm (2 in) in length in mid-summer, when the plants will have finished flowering, and again in early autumn, each time raking off the hay.

POND

A pond or wetland habitat is one of my favourites, attracting as it does frogs, toads, newts and dragonflies, and doubling up as a water-hole for mammals like foxes and hedgehogs.

I would suggest you make the pond as natural-looking as possible— created by excavating an irregular-shaped hole and lining it with butyl

How can one fail to be enticed to explore by this partly hidden path, flanked by summer-flowering shrubs and perennials?

rubber pool liner. It could, perhaps, be set in or at the edge of a mini-meadow, with the grass right up to the edge.

In the pool grow a selection of native aquatics like water iris, rushes and reed mace. The wet soil around the edge of the pond provides the ideal conditions for moisture-loving wild flowers like ragged robin, greater spearwort, meadow-sweet, purple loosestrife, hemp agrimony, devil's bit scabious and marsh marigold.

WOODLAND

A woodland habitat can be a charming feature in a garden and will attract all sorts of wildlife. If you have an area of woodland then devote part of it to a wildlife area by leaving it completely natural—don't clear anything out but allow fallen leaves and tree branches to rot naturally. Attractive wild flowers for the woodland habitat include primroses, violets and bluebells.

You must have a patch of stinging nettles somewhere in the garden for these encourage various butterflies such as the peacock, small tortoiseshell, red admiral, comma and painted lady. They lay their eggs on the nettles and their caterpillars feed on the leaves. Perhaps a good place for your nettle patch would be on the edge of the woodland habitat. Nettles do best in good rich soil so will appreciate the humus created by fallen leaves. Nettles spread rapidly in good conditions, so make sure you allow sufficient space for them.

HEDGEROW

A natural hedgerow attracts all kinds of wildlife and of course provides sanctuary and nesting sites for birds. An idea is to use a natural hedge as a boundary for a wildlife garden.

Form the hedge from native shrubs and trees, particularly those which provide food (berries and fruits) for birds, like hawthorn (*Crataegus monogyna*), the guelder rose (*Viburnum opulus*), the wayfaring tree (*Viburnum lantana*), the elder (*Sambucus nigra*), the mountain ash (*Sorbus aucuparia*) and dog rose (*Rosa canina*). Also allow the wild blackberry (*Rubus fruticosus*) to scramble through it, plus climbers like wild clematis (*Clematis vitalba*) and honeysuckle (*Lonicera periclymenum*). Collections of wild flower seeds suitable for the bottom of the hedgerow are readily available.

A HEATHER & CONIFER GARDEN

This is a modern idea, the aim of which is to provide colour throughout the year with minimum maintenance. An informal bed of heathers, with dwarf conifers set as specimens in it, looks particularly good in a lawn.

The heathers are planted in bold irregular groups to form a patchwork. On average, the planting density is five plants per square metre (square yard) for quick cover. This may need to be adjusted, though: very vigorous or spreading kinds may be better at three plants per square metre, while small-growing kinds may need to be set out at up to seven per square metre.

Remember that some heathers can only be grown in acid or lime-free soils, but there are others which will succeed in alkaline conditions.

A scheme for any soil

As an example of a planting scheme for acid or alkaline soils, I suggest featuring the winter-flowering heathers which do well on chalk. These flower throughout winter and into the spring. Most popular are the varieties of *Erica herbacea* (also known as *E. carnea*), like 'Springwood Pink' (pink flowers), 'Springwood White' (white), 'Myretoun Ruby' (ruby red) and 'Foxhollow' (lavender, but with brilliant gold foliage which is attractive all through the year). Varieties of the winter-flowering *Erica × darleyensis* are also highly recommended, like 'Arthur Johnson' (rose pink), 'Darley Dale' (pink) and 'Jack H. Brummage' (reddish purple).

The dwarf conifers I recommend for this scheme will provide colour all the year round. *Thuja occidentalis* 'Rheingold' has deep golden foliage; *Juniperus chinensis* 'Pyramidalis' is greyish or bluish green; *Chamaecyparis pisifera* 'Filifera Aurea' is brilliant yellow; and *Picea glauca* 'Albertiana Conica' bright green.

A scheme for acid soil

If you have an acid soil I can suggest the following scheme. The heathers bloom mainly in summer and winter and some have coloured foliage which is attractive all the year around. The foliage of the dwarf conifers will, likewise, provide interest throughout the year.

The heathers I recommend are *Erica × darleyensis* 'Silberschmelze' (white flowers, late autumn to mid-spring); *Calluna vulgaris* 'County Wicklow' (a pink ling, flowering late summer to early autumn); *Erica cinerea* 'Atrosanguinea Smith's Variety' (red flowers, early summer to early autumn); *Erica herbacea (E. carnea)* 'Vivellii' (carmine flowers, mid-winter to early spring); *Erica tetralix* 'Alba Mollis' (the cross-leaved heath, white flowers from early summer to early autumn and attractive silver-grey foliage); *Daboecia cantabrica* 'Praegerae' (St Daboec's heath, deep pink flowers from early summer to mid-autumn); *Calluna vulgaris* 'Robert Chapman' (purple flowers in late summer/early autumn and superb gold, bronze, red and yellow foliage); and *Erica vagans* 'Mrs D. F. Maxwell' (deep rose-pink flowers from late summer to mid-autumn).

Dwarf conifers which look well with this collection of heathers are *Chamaecyparis pisifera* 'Boulevard' (a superb silvery blue cone); *Thuja occidentalis* 'Rheingold' (a broad cone of deep gold foliage); and *Picea glauca* 'Albertiana Conica' (a bright green cone).

Heather and conifer beds are virtually maintenance free—all you need do is lightly trim over the heathers with shears after flowering to remove the dead blooms. Once the heathers are fully established and have completely covered the ground they will suppress annual weeds.

— A PAVED AREA FOR PLANTS —

Low carpeting and hummock-forming plants growing in gaps in random stone or crazy paving make an attractive informal feature for a country or cottage garden, although the idea could be used in town gardens, too.

The paving is laid on well-firmed soil (first eradicate all perennial weeds) and the joints filled with good gritty soil. Then an assortment of

plants is inserted in the joints and gaps. Alternatively you could plant as paving is being laid, which might make the job a bit easier for you.

There is no doubt that a natural stone such as York stone is best for this feature. It's expensive, but a small area should not completely empty the pocket. The feature should be sited in a sunny spot, for the majority of plants used are sun-lovers. And they like well-drained conditions so if your soil is on the heavy side incorporate plenty of grit or coarse horticultural sand to a depth of about 30 cm (12 in) before laying the paving.

Suitable plants

There are plenty of carpeting and neat hummock-forming plants to choose from, including alpines and dwarf shrubs. The following is a short selection of some of my favourites.

Thrift, or *Armeria caespitosa*, is a hummock-forming alpine studded with pink flowers in spring. 'Bevan's Variety' has flowers in a deeper shade. *A. maritima* is another good species with pink spring flowers, deep rose red in the variety 'Vindictive'.

Artemisia schmidtiana 'Nana' is a shrubby plant with mounds of silver-grey, finely cut foliage.

Ceratostigma plumbaginoides, a shrubby perennial, produces clusters of blue flowers from midsummer until well into autumn, when the leaves take on reddish tints.

Daphne cneorum, a prostrate evergreen spreading shrub, has rose-pink flowers in late spring/early summer. The variety 'Eximia' is also recommended.

Hebe rakaiensis, a small compact evergreen shrubby veronica, produces masses of white flowers in the summer. With bluish grey foliage is *H. pinguifolia* 'Pagei', which also has white flowers.

The rock roses, varieties of *Helianthemum nummularium*, are evergreen carpeting alpines bearing flowers like single roses in summer, in brilliant colours. There are lots of named varieties to choose from, including many with grey foliage.

Try the French lavender, *Lavandula stoechas*, with a mound of attractive grey-green foliage and deep purple flowers in summer, each spike crowned with a tuft of purple leaf-like bracts.

The carpeting species of knotweed, or polygonum, are ideally suited to growing in paving. I particularly recommend *Polygonum vacciniifolium* with small spikes of rose-red flowers from late summer to mid-autumn. I also recommend *P. affine* varieties 'Donald Lowndes' with rose-red flowers and 'Darjeeling Red' in deep pink, both flowering over a long period in summer.

The New Zealand raoulias are my great favourites. They are alpines, forming prostrate mats of tiny evergreen leaves. *Raoulia australis* (also known as *R. hookeri*) forms a silvery mat; *R. glabra* is bright green; and *R. lutescens* is grey-green and in spring liberally sprinkled with tiny yellow flowers.

The ornamental sages I value for their aromatic foliage. They are varieties of *Salvia officinalis*: 'Icterina' with gold-variegated leaves, 'Purpurascens' with purple-flushed foliage, and 'Tricolor' whose leaves are splashed with white and have purple and pink tints.

The houseleeks or sempervivums are excellent low hummock-forming

Opposite: A wrought-iron gate gives tantalizing glimpses of the garden beyond. The gate is framed with a large, mature wisteria.

alpines for paving and will grow in the poorest conditions. They form rosettes of succulent leaves. There are dozens of varieties to choose from. I particularly like the cobweb houseleek, though, *S. arachnoideum*, with web-like hairs; and *S. tectorum* 'Commander Hay' with shiny purple, green-tipped leaves.

Finally I must mention the mat-forming thymes whose aromatic foliage gives off a delightful scent when the plants are trodden on (although do not make a habit of this!). They are varieties of *Thymus serpyllum* (also known as *T. drucei*) and include 'Albus' with white flowers; 'Annie Hall', pale pink; 'Coccineus', crimson; and 'Lanuginosus', a great favourite of mine, with grey woolly leaves and lilac flowers.

A ROCK GARDEN

For many years rock gardens have been popular garden features providing suitable and natural-looking habitats for alpine plants. Probably the earliest rock garden in England was that made at the Chelsea Physic Garden, in London, in 1772. It consists of old stone from the Tower of London, Icelandic lava, chalk and flints simply placed in a heap. It still exists and quite honestly is a monstrosity—in no way does it imitate nature, as we try to do today. There followed many similar examples over the years—heaps of stones assembled for their own sake rather than for the growing of plants. By about the middle of the last century, though, natural-looking rock gardens, resembling outcrops of rock, were being built and suitably planted. By the late nineteenth century there was great interest in cultivating alpine plants and it has never waned to this day.

If you have a bank, that's the ideal site for a natural-looking rock garden, for on it you can build a series of step-like outcrops with level planting beds between them (details of rock-garden construction will be found in Chapter 6). In this type of rock garden you can, of course, have a waterfall running through it and into a pool at the bottom.

A rock garden can be built on flat ground if you do not have a bank. Rocks can be partially sunk into the soil to form several small natural-looking outcrops (again, see Chapter 6 for construction details). You could have gravel or natural stone paths weaving between the outcrops. On no account when building a rock garden on the flat be tempted to form a mound of soil and place rocks on it—this typifies rock-garden construction of a couple of centuries ago and such a monstrosity is mockingly known as a 'dog's grave'. You would never find such an object in nature.

In nature one often finds masses of rock emerging from the ground (outcrops) and this has been achieved by the weather eroding the soil to expose the rock below. This is the effect we should be trying to achieve.

For this reason, one should buy local rock as this is more in keeping than buying rock which is totally alien to your part of the country. (And besides it keeps down transport costs!) Buy reasonably large pieces of rock (pieces that you are able to move, though!), all of roughly similar size and more or less rectangular in shape.

The rock garden should be in an open sunny position as most alpines are sun-lovers.

Planting ideas

A rock garden can be planted with alpines or rock plants of your choice –there are hundreds to choose from. Trailing kinds can be planted to cascade over the edges of rocks, and in vertical joints between rocks. Hummock-forming kinds can be planted in the level beds. I will not attempt to recommend a selection of alpines as there are so many to choose from.

Remember that miniature bulbs should be planted, too, for providing colour in late winter and spring. The main flowering period of alpines is spring, but on the other hand many bloom in summer, so make sure you plant some for that season as well, to ensure continuity of colour. Alpines grown for their foliage, like sempervivums (houseleeks), raoulias and sedums should also be included for autumn/winter colour and interest.

You should include some small shrubs and dwarf conifers, too, for contrast in height and habit. One of the best dwarf conifers for a small rock garden is a juniper, *Juniperus communis* 'Compressa', which forms a tiny cone. Suitable small shrubs include *Cytisus ardoinii* (broom), *Daphne collina*, *Jasminum parkeri* (jasmine), *Salix lanata* (woolly willow) and *Spiraea japonica* 'Bullata'. Shrubs which must have acid soil include dwarf rhododendrons and *Andromeda polifolia* 'Compacta' which like moisture-retentive peaty soil.

On no account position upright shrubs and cone- or bun-shaped conifers at the top of a rock garden as they look ridiculous–place them on the lower levels. Prostrate shrubs and conifers, though, do look at home at the top. This imitates nature–you don't see tall trees near the top of a mountain, but rather very dwarf scrubby specimens. After planting a rock garden it is usual to cover the surface of the beds with stone chippings or pea shingle, not only to give a more natural appearance, but also to help suppress annual weeds and conserve moisture during dry periods.

A GRASSY ROCK GARDEN

The type of rock garden I have described is, nevertheless, labour-intensive. Even with a covering of stone chippings some weeding is necessary and this has to be done by hand. Plants of many kinds will need trimming over, even if only to remove dead flowers.

If you feel all of this is a bit too much, then why not opt for a completely natural rock garden? In nature, especially on downland and hills, rock outcrops are surrounded by grass, often kept short by grazing sheep. In a garden setting semi-long grass between and around rock outcrops can be extremely pleasing and will only need cutting a few times a year (you could use a nylon cord trimmer to speed up the job). Use a fine grass-seed mixture, containing fescues, as this gives a better effect than coarse-leaved grasses like ryegrass. Here we are going back to the original idea of using rocks for their own sake. I have seen this done and can assure you it can be most effective.

A SCREE BED

During the evolution of rock gardens gradually fewer rocks were used for building. Today there are several compact and economical ways of providing suitable conditions for alpines, including the currently popular scree bed.

In nature a scree is a drift of broken rock at the base of a rock face or cliff. This layer of rock particles does not retain much moisture as it has little soil or humus in it.

In the garden we construct a scree so that it is very free draining. It is, therefore, suitable for many choice alpines which need such conditions.

A scree bed provides a good way of growing alpines in a small garden, as it does not have to be large, and it looks good with modern architecture —indeed in a modern setting a scree bed probably looks more in keeping than a proper rock garden which, after all, is a very informal feature.

First you have to build a raised bed, which can be any shape and size desired. Depth, however, is important to ensure an ample layer of drainage material in the base. The bed can be about 30 cm (12 in) deep if your garden soil is already very well drained; it should be about 60 cm (24 in) deep if your soil is badly drained.

It should be sited in an open sunny spot, as for rock gardens, for most alpines are sun lovers. The bed can be built up with natural walling stone. You could build a dry-stone wall, with soil in the joints, in which to plant trailing alpines. Or it could be build up with bricks or ornamental concrete walling blocks, bonded with mortar. Plenty of drainage holes must be included all round at the base of the walls.

Place a layer of rubble or broken bricks in the bottom to ensure good drainage. This can be about 10 cm (4 in) deep if the garden soil is naturally well drained; or at least 15 cm (6 in) if the soil is badly drained. Top this with a layer of partially decomposed leaves to prevent compost from washing down into it.

Then fill up with a well-drained compost consisting of 10 parts stone chippings or pea shingle, 1 part loam, 1 part peat and 1 part sharp horticultural sand. Add a little organic slow-release fertilizer such as bonemeal. Add one or two well-shaped pieces of rock, partially sunk into the compost, to create an attractive appearance.

Selection of plants

There are plenty of alpines which revel in the conditions provided by a scree bed. Try the following (some species of many of these genera are really choice plants and need cosseting): *Androsace, Calceolaria, Daphne, Dianthus, Draba, Gentiana, Hebe, Iris, Leontopodium (edelweiss), Lewisia, Phyteuma,* many saxifrages (*Saxifraga*), *Sedum, Teucrium* and *Veronica*.

—— A GARDEN OF STONE SINKS ——

Another very compact and economical way of growing alpines is in stone or simulated-stone sinks, which is quite a modern idea.

The sinks can be grouped together on a paved or gravel area where they provide an attractive and somewhat unusual feature. Again, an open sunny site should be chosen.

If you can obtain genuine old shallow stone sinks then you are indeed fortunate, for they are now very scarce and considered collectors' items—and expensive.

Fortunately, though, one can convert the ubiquitous white glazed sink. Carefully done, and when well weathered, it can look like a genuine stone sink.

The white glazed sink is covered with a mixture of cement, sand and peat, known as hypertufa, which, when hard and weathered, resembles natural tufa rock.

First the sink has to be treated with a PVA adhesive (as used in the building trade, and available from DIY and hardware stores). Brush it on the outside of the sink and also part way down the inside. When the adhesive has become tacky (before it is fully dry) apply the hypertufa mix.

A hypertufa mix consists of 2 parts sphagnum peat, 1 part sand and 1 part cement–parts by volume. Sufficient water should be added to make a stiff but pliable mix. This is spread about 12 mm ($\frac{1}{2}$ in) thick over the treated parts of the sink, firmly pressing it into place. You can leave a fairly rough texture, to resemble natural stone. The hypertufa will take at least a couple

A well-planted water garden can make a colourful and interesting garden feature. The moist surrounds of this one are planted with primulas, irises, ferns, hostas and other choice plants.

79

of weeks to harden thoroughly. Before planting the sink I suggest that you block the drainage hole and then fill it with a solution of permanganate of potash. Leave for about 24 hours. This will remove any chemicals, which may be harmful to plants, from the cement. Then thoroughly wash out with clean water.

Add a layer of broken clay flower pots in the bottom of the sink (with one large piece over the drainage hole) about 2.5 cm (1 in) deep, to act as a drainage layer, and top with a thin layer of rough peat or leafmould. The sink is then filled to within 2.5 cm (1 in) of the top with potting compost. I generally use a soil-based compost but add to it one-third extra of coarse horticultural sand or grit to ensure really good drainage. Add one or two small well-shaped pieces of rock, partially sinking them into the compost. Then you are ready for planting.

Usually sinks are slightly raised above ground level and this is easily achieved before filling by setting them on two rows of bricks—two courses make a good height. They can be bonded with mortar to ensure stability.

Suitable alpines

Coming on to suitable alpines for sink gardens, I think one or two dwarf conifers are useful for giving contrast in height and form. The most suitable, as it is the smallest and exceedingly slow growing, is *Juniperus communis* 'Compressa' which makes a tiny greyish cone.

Trailing alpines are recommended for the edges of the sink, like *Phlox douglasii*, with lilac flowers in spring, and *Aethionema armenum*, with pink flowers in early summer. The silvery leaved *Raoulia hookeri* (syn. *R. australis*) will also help to soften the edges as it has a spreading habit of growth.

Other suitably restrained alpines include the thrift, *Armeria caespitosa*, with pink flowers in spring; the rock pink, *Dianthus neglectus*, rose pink blooms in early summer; *Geranium cinereum*, pink blooms in spring; the white, early summer-flowering *Gypsophila caucasica*; various saxifrages, such as *Saxifraga × burseriana*, white blooms, spring; and the cobweb houseleek, *Sempervivum arachnoideum*, whose leaves are densely covered with white hairs, like spiders' webs. There are lots more alpines which are suitable for sink gardens. Make sure, though, you do not plant vigorous or rampant growers which would soon take over the entire sink. After planting cover the surface of the compost with a layer of stone chippings or pea single, for the sake of appearance and to ensure good drainage around the plants.

— ISLAND BEDS FOR PERENNIALS —

Growing hardy perennials in island beds, using plants which need minimum attention and no staking, is quite a modern idea and replaces the traditional labour-intensive herbaceous border. The idea was pioneered by Alan Bloom, of Bressingham Gardens, a leading authority on hardy perennials.

Ideally one should have a group of informal beds, with gently curving edges, set in a lawn or a paved or gravelled area, with paths between them so that thay can be viewed from all sides. A group of three beds looks particularly pleasing, if you have the space, but for small gardens a single bed still makes an attractive feature.

Hardy perennials for island beds—which should be set in an open sunny position—should be self-supporting and not excessively vigorous. A collection of plants should be capable of providing colour from spring to autumn, peaking in the summer.

Each variety should be planted in a bold informal group, ideally at least one square metre (square yard) in area, so that a bold effect is created. Therefore you will need several plants of each variety—say from three to five, depending on vigour.

The tallest plants are set in the centre of each bed, grading down to shorter ones at the edges, so that all plants can be seen. However, do not be too rigid in this respect, as it can create an unnatural, regimented appearance. One or two groups of short plants can be extended towards the centre of the bed, and a group or two of intermediate plants can be extended towards the edge of the bed.

Try to group plants for contrast in flower and foliage shape. For example, you could group plants with spikes of flowers with those which produce blooms in flat heads; or combine plants with grassy or sword-like foliage with those which have bold, rounded leaves. Don't forget to consider colours, too, grouping plants which contrast or harmonize pleasantly.

There is a vast range of plants to choose from but the following is a good representative selection.

Plants for spring colour

Adonis amurensis 'Fukujukai', yellow flowers, ferny leaves; *Dicentra formosa* 'Bountiful', purplish crimson, ferny foliage; *Dicentra spectabilis,* red heart-shaped flowers, ferny foliage; *Doronicum* 'Spring Beauty' and 'Miss Mason', yellow daisy flowers; *Euphorbia epithymoides*, lime-green flowers; *Pulmonaria angustifolia*, brilliant pure blue; *Ranunculus gramineus* a grassy-leaved buttercup with yellow flowers; and *Trollius × cultorum* varieties with globe-shaped flowers in yellow or orange.

Plants for summer colour

Acanthus spinosus, deeply cut leaves and spikes of purple and white flowers; *Alchemilla mollis*, mounds of lime-green flowers; *Anthemis tinctoria* 'Mrs Buxton' and 'Wargrave' with yellow daisy flowers; *Campanula glomerata* 'Superba', bell-shaped violet flowers; *Coreopsis verticillata* 'Grandiflora', yellow daisy flowers; *Erigeron*, many varieties, with daisy-like flowers in blues, pinks etc; *Euphorbia griffithii* 'Fireglow', brilliant orange-red flowers; *Geranium endressii* varieties with pink flowers; *Helenium* hybrids like coppery orange 'Coppelia' and bronze-red 'Moerheim Beauty'; *Iris pallida* 'Variegata', sword-like cream and green leaves; *Liatris* 'Kobold', spikes of deep lilac flowers; *Linum narbonnense*, bright blue; *Lysimachia clethroides*, curved spikes of white flowers; *Monarda didyma* varieties like 'Cambridge Scarlet' and 'Croftway Pink'; *Oenothera* 'Highlight', large yellow saucer-shaped flowers; *Penstemon* hybrids with tubular flowers in shades of red and blue; *Phlox paniculata* varieties in shades of pink, red, orange, blue, etc; *Salvia superba* varieties like 'East Friesland', 'Lubeca' and 'May Night' with spikes of violet-purple flowers; *Stachys macrantha* 'Superba', spikes of mauve-lilac flowers; and *Veronica gentianoides* with spikes of light blue flowers.

Paths disappearing from view help to link one part of the garden with another, this one leading to a secluded sitting area. The path is formed of random stone — most appropriate in this informal setting.

Plants for autumn colour

Anemone hybrida 'Bressingham Glow', large rounded rose-red flowers; *Aster novi-belgii* varieties, especially the dwarf varieties like 'Lady in Blue' and 'Little Pink Beauty'; *Liriope muscari*, grassy leaves and spikes of violet-mauve flowers; *Polygonum affine* varieties like 'Darjeeling Red' and 'Donald Lowndes' with small spikes of pink flowers; *Sedum* 'Autumn Joy', flat heads of salmon-pink flowers; *Solidago* or golden rod, especially dwarf varieties like 'Cloth of Gold' and 'Golden Thumb' with yellow flowers; and *Stokesia laevis*, with large blue daisy flowers, deep blue in the variety 'Wyoming'.

PEAT BED

This is a raised bed filled with a peaty soil mixture for plants that need acid, moist spongy soil. It's an ideal feature if you have alkaline soil in your garden and want to grow lime-hating plants. The peat bed is a modern idea, probably more popular in the USA than in Britain and, like the scree, it is suitable for a modern garden.

Instead of a bed on flat ground, a peat garden could be tiered on a bank (a series of terraces). But whatever design you choose, the peat bed must be in shade, for the plants are shade-lovers. The dappled shade cast by trees or large shrubs is also suitable for peat-garden plants.

There is no reason, of course, why a peat bed should not be built on naturally acid soil. The plants will benefit from the very peaty moist compost that the bed should contain. Many acid soils are sandy and dry out rapidly in summer, which is no good for the plants that I have in mind.

The bed can be any size or shape desired—in my opinion the more informal the better. It must have a minimum depth of 30 cm (12 in), which would be suitable for acid garden soils. But if your soil is alkaline I would recommend a greater depth to ensure that plants do not root into the soil below—hence a minimum depth of 45 cm (18 in).

The bed (or terraces on a bank) is built up with peat blocks. These are

Here a gravel path disappears from view, being flanked with old-fashioned shrub roses, foxgloves, poppies and other summer flowers – truly an English garden.

brick-sized blocks of peat which are sold in dry form. They must be moistened before use by soaking them for at least 24 hours in a tank of water. Peat blocks should be bonded or staggered, just like brickwork, when building up the walls. The walls of the bed or terraces should tilt slightly inwards for stability. As you lay the blocks fill the joints with compost (see formula below), as you would use mortar when laying bricks.

Before filling the bed with compost place an 8 cm (3 in) deep layer of rough peat in the bottom, directly over the bare soil. Then fill with a compost consisting of 4 parts moist sphagnum peat, 1 part fibrous acid loam and 1 part lime-free coarse sand (parts by volume). After planting topdress the surface of the compost with sphagnum peat and top it up annually in the spring. During dry weather keep the peat blocks watered to prevent them drying out and shrinking.

Suitable plants

All plants should be dwarf or fairly small, and restrained in spread, so that they do not outgrow the bed.

Arctostaphyllos uva-ursi is a prostrate evergreen shrub which does have quite a wide spread, but to overcome this problem plant it near the edge of the bed so that it spreads over the edge. It produces white urn-shaped flowers in the spring followed by red berries.

Cassiope lycopodioides and *C. tetragona* are small evergreen shrubs with white bell-like flowers in spring. Gaultherias are suitable, too, provided you pick small-growing kinds like *G. trichophylla*. This is another small evergreen shrub, with deep pink urn-shaped flowers in spring followed by blue berries.

Lithospermum diffusum is a small sub-shrub with the most gorgeous pure blue flowers produced between early summer and mid-autumn. A good variety is 'Heavenly Blue'.

You may have difficulty in finding a supplier of *Ourisia coccinea*, as it is certainly not freely available. However, I feel I must list it for this is one of the most beautiful peat-garden plants. A small perennial, it bears from late spring to early autumn scarlet tubular flowers on upright stems.

Philesia magellanica is a dwarf evergreen shrub suited to outdoor cultivation only in mild areas as it is not too hardy. It produces in spring and early summer waxy rose-red bell-like flowers similar to those of lapageria, to which it is related.

The heath-like dwarf evergreen shrub *Phyllodoce aleutica* produces globular greeny yellow flowers in spring and early summer. There are many dwarf species of rhododendron for the peat bed and they flower in the spring or early summer. *R. impeditum* forms a small mound of tiny leaves and produces purplish blue flowers. *R. forrestii repens* is a small prostrate plant with scarlet bell-shaped flowers. *R. campylogynum* has waxy bell-shaped blooms which may be pink or purplish, depending on the form obtained. *R. keiskei* comes into flower in early spring and has trusses of lemon yellow funnel-shaped flowers.

Finally small vacciniums are a good choice for the peat garden, like *V. praestans* with a prostrate creeping habit and white or reddish bell-shaped flowers in early summer, followed by red berries and brilliant autumn leaf colour.

6
MAKING AND PLANTING

Many garden features have been described in previous chapters but with most I have not given guidance on how to build or plant them. So I am devoting this chapter to the practical aspects of creating features.

GARDEN HARDWARE

Professionals call this 'hard landscaping', which embraces the building of walls, the erection of fences and other screens, the laying of paths and patios, the building of rock gardens, the creation of pools and so on. I will consider all of these features, and more besides. Hopefully you will find this a fascinating and rewarding aspect of garden making.

WALLS

Foundations
Walls must be built on substantial foundations to prevent them from sinking or even falling over! All walls can be built on a trench foundation. Take out a trench and fill it with well-rammed hardcore and concrete. The foundation should be wider that the wall: the width should equal at least the depth of the concrete. The depth of the hardcore should be of the same depth as the concrete. For a wall over six courses of bricks high (which is applicable to most of the walls I have described) you should take out a trench 50 cm (20 in) deep. This will, therefore, have 25 cm (10 in) of hardcore in the bottom, topped by 25 cm of concrete. A concrete mix for foundations consists of 1 part cement and 5 parts all-in aggregate.

Planning permission
Planning permission is needed from your local authority for a boundary wall over 1 m (3 ft 3 in) high alongside a public highway; or 2 m (6 ft 6 in) high inside the garden. This, of course, is mainly for safety reasons – walls must comply with local building regulations.

Brick walls
Dwarf walls, up to 60 cm (2 ft) high, can be only one brick thick. Walls over 60 cm high should be two bricks thick; and when a wall of over 1.8 m (6 ft) is being considered, it should be three bricks thick. Usually an acceptable maximum height for a wall is 1.8 m. If you want to go over this, however, or want an exceptionally long wall, you should seek professional advice as it may well need special reinforcement, such as buttresses.

Bricks (or ornamental concrete walling blocks) must overlap to create a staggered bond, or pattern, for rigidity. Examples of bonding are shown in Fig. 11.

The stretcher bond is very simple, but only suitable for walls which are one brick thick. The bricks are laid end to end but overlap by half on alternate courses. Open brickwork walls are also one brick thick.

For walls which are to be two bricks thick you could have courses of stretchers (bricks laid end to end) alternating with courses of headers (bricks laid across the width of the wall). Flemish bond brickwork is also recommended for double-thickness walls.

A garden wall should have a damp-proof course of low-water absorption bricks. These can form the first two courses.

First, build up the wall at each end (Fig. 12). Then fill in the middle where, if necessary, bricks can be cut. Mortar for brick laying consists of 1 part cement and 6 parts builders' sand. Use tight strings as a guide to keep courses straight, and check vertical and horizontal alignment regularly with a spirit level.

A secluded patio, complete with raised bed and well-planted ornamental containers. The emphasis is on foliage plants, but geraniums provide splashes of colour in the summer (garden designer: Mackenzie Bell).

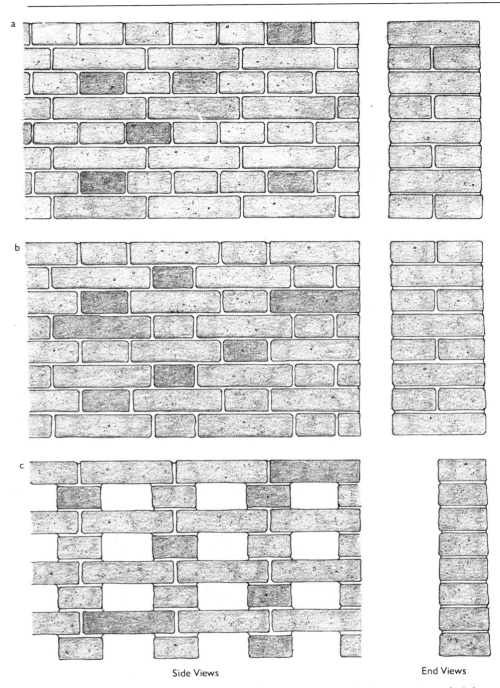

a

b

c

Side Views   End Views

Fig. 11. *Examples of brick bonding. English bond (a) consists of courses of stretchers alternating with courses of headers. Flemish bond brickwork (b) is also recommended for double-thickness walls. Open-brickwork walls (c) help to prevent a 'shut-in' effect.*

Press the mortar joints, when partially set, into a V shape, using a bricklaying trowel.

Finally coping should be placed on top of the wall to deflect rain and there should be a damp-proof course immediately below it. You can use special bricks for this, or coping stones. Use capping stones for any pillars you may have constructed.

Screen-block walls

These are built from concrete blocks with an openwork pattern. Each block measures 30 by 30 by 10 cm (12 by 12 by 4 in) and they cannot be cut. There

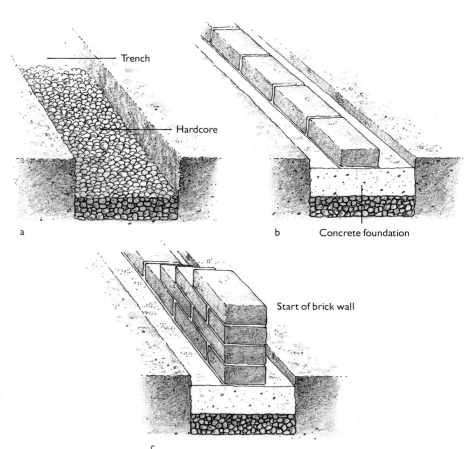

Trench

Hardcore

a

Concrete foundation

b

Start of brick wall

c

Fig. 12. *Building a wall. Start with a trench for the foundations, partially filled with well-rammed hardcore (a). Top the hardcore with a similar depth of concrete (b). Build up the wall at each end (c), then fill in the middle.*

are no half sizes, either. A screen-block wall is built up in stack bond (one block above the other) as shown in Fig 13. Usually screen-block walls have a maximum height of 1.8 m (6 ft).

A screen-block wall is supported with piers spaced 1.8–3 m (6–10 ft) apart. These are formed from hollow cubes known as pilasters, which have slots in them into which the blocks are locked. Steel reinforcing rods are positioned through the centre of each pier, the bases of the rods being bedded in the concrete foundation. Fill the piers with concrete during building.

Finish off a screen-block wall with coping and pilaster cappings.

Retaining walls

These are walls which are built against a bank to retain the soil – or indeed in any other situation where soil has to be supported, such as the walling in a sunken garden or the walls supporting a terrace.

Where a wall is to receive a lot of pressure it is best built with bricks to three bricks in thickness. If it is to be over 1.2 m (4 ft) high you are advised to seek professional advice on building. Drainage holes should be provided in the base of the wall.

A dry-stone retaining wall is attractive: it is formed of natural stone, laid without mortar. Usually it is kept low – 1 m (3 ft) or less – and should slope slightly into the bank for stability. It should tilt back, though, only on the outer face, so that the wall is in fact wedge shaped, vertical at the back. A slope of 5 cm in 30 cm (2 in in 1 ft) is adequate. The bank should be cut so that it has a vertical face, against which the wall is built.

The stones are laid at random but should be interlocked to ensure a really strong wall. Ties should be inserted at intervals to hold the wall securely into the bank. Place large wide stones across the wall and into the bank.

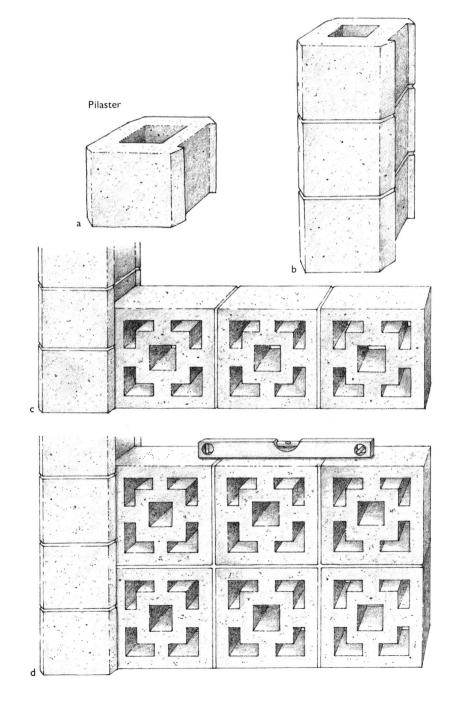

Pilaster

a

b

c

d

Fig. 13. *A screen-block wall. This should be supported with piers formed from hollow cubes known as pilasters (a). The piers (b) have metal reinforcing rods through them. The concrete blocks are locked into the slots of the pilasters (c) during building. Blocks are laid in stack bond – one above the other (d).*

Soil should be placed between joints and the soil behind the wall packed firmly as building proceeds.

Large flat stones should be placed on top of the wall to act as coping.

FENCES AND SCREENS

Posts

Substantial timber posts are needed to support fences and trelliswork screens. Buy square fencing posts 8 cm (3 in) square and, if not already treated, 'paint' them with horticultural timber preservative. It pays to soak the ends of the posts in preservative overnight.

The easiest way to insert posts is to use proprietary metal post supports (Fig. 14) which are simply hammered into the ground. A metal post support consists of a strong steel spike with a square 'box' at the top, into which the post is pushed once the support has been inserted in the ground. Some metal post supports have a box which can be adjusted in any plane to ensure correct positioning of the post. Some also have a double bolting arrangement to ensure really secure post fixing. Then there are metal post supports

Fig. 14. The easiest way to insert fencing posts is to use proprietary metal post supports (a). The support is hammered into the ground (b) using a protective cap. The post is then pushed into the support, some of which can be tightened with bolts (c).

designed for concreting into the ground when it is not possible to use the spiked type, or where the soil is too light to hold the latter adequately.

Alternatively, the wooden posts can be concreted directly into the ground. You will need to take out holes 60 cm (2 ft) deep for fences over 1.2 m (4 ft) in height, and holes 45 cm (18 in) deep for lower fences. Remove an extra 15 cm (6 in) depth of soil and replace with 15 cm of rammed hardcore to act as a drainage layer.

Then wedge each post upright in the centre of the hole and fill in to soil level with a slightly moist concrete mix (1 part cement to 4 parts all-in aggregate).

The tops of the posts should be provided with wooden caps.

A natural arch in a hedge frames these phloxes in the herbaceous border beyond. What other treats does the border have to offer?

For screening purposes fences and trelliswork (Fig 15) should be about 1.8 m (6 ft) high. You will therefore need 1.8 m posts if you use metal post supports, or 2.4 m (8 ft) posts if they are to be concreted into the ground.

Prefabricated fencing panels

To erect these lapped or interwoven panels, first insert a post at one end. Secure a panel to it with 8 cm (3 in) galvanized nails. Then insert the next post and nail the panel to that. Fix the second panel to this post. Continue in this way, noting that the panels are held *between* the posts.

Ranch-type fencing and wattle panels

With ranch-type fencing the horizontal bars are nailed to the front of the posts, using 8 cm (3 in) galvanized nails. Wattle panels are secured in the same way.

Close-boarded timber fencing

This is constructed from scratch, on site. It can be put up by a fencing specialist, or you may wish to make it yourself.

Arris rails (the horizontal rails) are mortised into the posts as the latter are erected. Two to three rails will be needed. Next, horizontal gravel boards – 15 by 2.5 cm (6 by 1 in) – are nailed to cleats at the base of the posts.

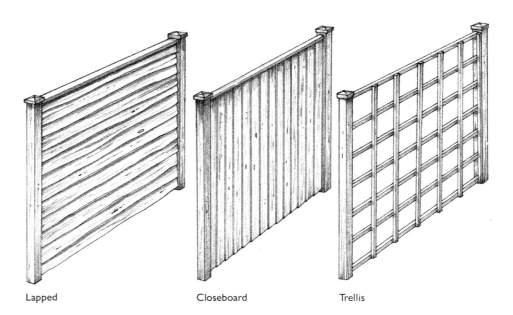

Lapped   Closeboard   Trellis

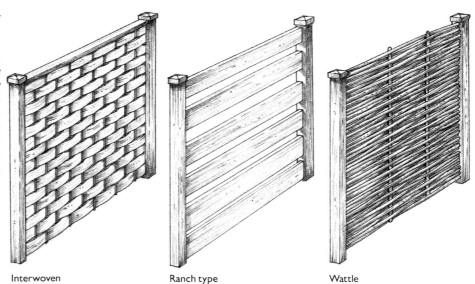

Fig. 15. *Fencing can be a reasonably economic method of dividing a garden and there are several styles to choose from. Prefabricated lapped panels look good in both town and country gardens. Close-boarded timber is also recommended for any setting. Trelliswork screens do not seriously reduce light, nor do they result in a boxed-in effect. Prefabricated interwoven panels are popular with town and country gardeners. Ranch-type fencing is often used in modern town gardens and is generally painted white. Wattle fencing panels are made from hazelwood and look particularly good in country or cottage gardens.*

Interwoven   Ranch type   Wattle

The vertical feather-edged boards which are used for this type of fencing should overlap by 12 mm ($\frac{1}{2}$ in) and sit on top of the gravel board. They are nailed to the arris rails, using galvanized nails. Finally nail a wooden coping strip on top of the fence.

Trelliswork screens
These come in panel form and are erected in the same way as prefabricated fencing panels.

PAVING

Various patterns which can be created with pre-cast concrete paving slabs and bricks are shown in Fig. 16. Whether you use these to make a patio, terrace etc., or opt for concrete, you will first need to lay an adequate foundation.

Foundations
First level the soil and then thoroughly consolidate it. Place on top a 10 cm (4 in) layer of hardcore and ram this down well, too. Cover the hardcore with a 4 cm (1$\frac{1}{2}$ in) layer of soft builders' sand to fill in holes and gaps and to create a smooth level surface on which to lay your paving material.

Laying paving slabs
Pre-cast concrete paving slabs and square or retangular natural-stone slabs are best spot-bedded on mortar (1 part cement, 6 parts sand), five pads of mortar for each slab.

Gently tap down each slab to ensure it is level. Leave 6 mm ($\frac{1}{4}$ in) joints between the slabs and later grout them with mortar. This is most easily achieved by filling them with dry mortar mix and then moistening it with the aid of a rosed watering can.

Laying bricks
These are best laid loosely (not on mortar) as then they are easily replaced if they become damaged. Lay them flat rather than on edge, leaving 9 mm ($\frac{3}{8}$ in) joints which are then filled with sand. Bricks which are used to edge a patio, etc, are best bedded on mortar for stability.

Laying concrete
It is best not to lay concrete during frosty weather. First erect timber shuttering to the shape of the area to be concreted, not forgetting any beds that are to be included in the area. Use stout timber planks and nail them to wooden posts inserted firmly into the ground. The top of the shuttering should be at the level required for the surface of the concrete.

The concrete can be laid 8 cm (3 in) thick. Make up a mix of 1 part cement and 5 parts all-in aggregate, or buy ready-mixed concrete. Tamp it down well–for example, with a long wooden plank on edge (Fig. 17), with another person at the other end if necessary. For very small areas, the back of a rake may be used to tamp down the concrete.

To create a textured surface lightly brush the concrete with a stiff brush when it has partially set to expose the aggregate.

A secluded, leafy corner with a rich tapestry of foliage plants, while overhead a white climbing rose flowers.

If you are laying a large area of concrete you should provide expansion joints, about 12 mm ($\frac{1}{2}$ in) wide. Lay the concrete in 3 m (10 ft) square sections.

After laying concrete cover it with a sheet of polythene to keep rain off and to allow it to dry out slowly. You should be able to walk on it after five days if it is laid in summer, or after 10 days if it is laid in winter. Do not subject concrete to heavy use for at least two weeks after laying, at which time the shuttering can safely be removed.

Cobbles and granite setts
It is best to bed cobbles and granite setts in mortar to prevent movement.

Generally only small areas are laid with these materials, usually to act as a contrast to an area of paving slabs.

Random-stone paving

There are two ways of laying natural random-stone or 'crazy' paving but in both cases fairly wide joints are left—up to 2.5 cm (1 in) or so. If you want to grow plants in the paving then lay it on well-rammed earth and fill the joints with gritty soil. If you don't want plants in the paving then it can be laid as for concrete paving slabs, on a substantial foundation, filling the joints with mortar. In this instance you will have no trouble from weeds growing in the joints; the former can be time consuming to remove.

A path leads through a veritable tunnel of foliage, encouraging one to explore. Note the focal point – a classical tub of purple pansies.

95

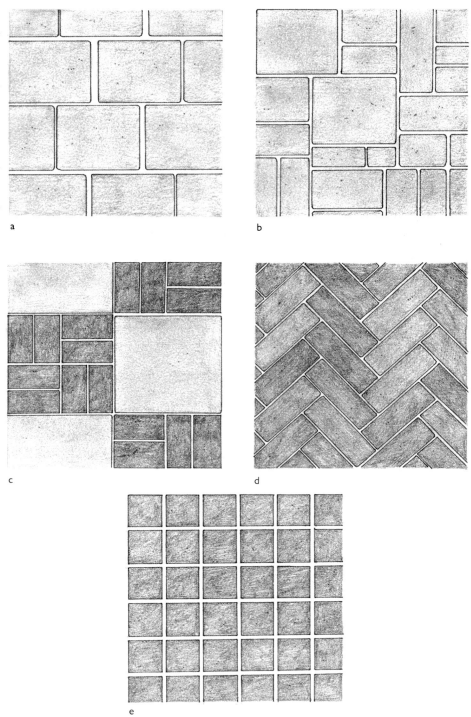

Fig. 16. *Various patterns which can be created with pre-cast concrete paving slabs and bricks. Gaps between slabs can be varied (a) if you do not want a very formal effect. Quite an informal effect can be achieved by using slabs in various sizes and shades (b). A marvellous combination consists of a mix-ture of concrete slabs and bricks (c). Bricks can be laid in a herringbone pattern (d). Small quarry tiles (e) might be more suitable for paving in some situations, such as in a small courtyard.*

PATHS

For aesthetic as well as practical reasons paths should not be too narrow. Even in a small garden a path should not be less than 60 cm (2 ft) wide, while in large gardens paths 1–1.2 m (3–4 ft) wide are more in proportion.

Materials

Many of the materials described under Paving can be used for paths and these are laid in exactly the same way, again on substantial foundations. If you choose concrete (Fig. 17), make sure you leave expansion joints every 2 m (6 ft) and a rough-textured, non-slip surface. Pre-cast concrete paving slabs, random stone (but try to maintain straight edges to the path) or bricks are also suitable. For informal gardens gravel makes a good path (see below) and should be retained by boards or curbing along each edge of the path. The same applies to pulverized bark, which makes a soft mud-free path and is especially recommended for woodland areas. Bark should be laid about 5 cm (2 in) deep.

Stepping stones

Stepping stones are highly recommended for informal gardens but they can also be effectively incorporated into formal gardens if square, circular or hexagonal paving slabs are used. Random stone is better in an informal area, as are sections of tree trunk. Stepping stones are often very pleasing when used across a lawn.

There is no need for a lot of preparation prior to laying stepping stones –indeed, they are generally laid directly on firmed soil. Set them 15–22 cm (6–9 in) apart.

Simply cut out a suitable sized hole for each stone, in the lawn or soil, set the stone in place after firming the ground and then firm the soil all round. Stepping stones should be just below the surface of a lawn so that the mower can pass over them. It is most important to take care that the stones are firmly bedded, to preclude the risk of movement later on.

GRAVEL AREAS

Pea shingle is generally used to create gravel areas and is laid directly on to well consolidated soil. If you want to ensure the soil becomes really firm (for instance, if you have a light sandy soil) then mix some dry cement into the surface before ramming it. Do not use cement, though, for any areas which you intend to plant,

The pea shingle should be spread evenly over the prepared site, but not more than 2.5 cm (1 in) deep. If deeper than this it is difficult to walk on–your heels will sink into it. The area should be edged with wooden boards, small curbing stones or bricks partially sunk into the soil, to prevent the gravel from spreading.

It is advisable to eradicate all perennial weeds before you start preparing the site, as gravel will not suppress these. So several months beforehand spray them, when they are in full growth, with a weedkiller containing glyphosate, according to the manufacturer's instructions.

Weeds will, of course, eventually appear in a gravel area but they are easily controlled by spraying with a proprietary path weedkiller.

STEPS

Garden steps should not be made too steep. The risers (the vertical parts) should be 15 cm (6 in) high, and the treads (the parts that you walk on)

should be a minimum of 30 cm (12 in) deep and ideally up to 45 cm (18 in) deep. Steps should not be less than 90 cm (3 ft) wide.

As with paving and paths, it is best to build steps on a foundation of well-rammed hardcore to ensure they remain really stable.

Concrete steps

These are quite easy to build, using half risers of rectangular stones, building blocks or bricks (laid flat), as shown in Fig. 18.

The concrete is laid 8 cm (3 in) deep, so the risers will have to be built to a height of 8 cm to give a 15 cm (6 in) rise. For details of the concrete mix, and laying, refer to the section on Paving.

Start by roughly excavating the shape of the steps in the bank. Then lay the first riser, on a concrete foundation for stability. Always bed the stones, bricks etc., on mortar to hold them firm.

Cover the tread area behind the riser with hardcore, and ram it down well, ensuring it is level with the top of the riser.

Next, install wooden shuttering across the front of the riser, to a height of 8 cm (3 in) above it. Also install shuttering at the back of the tread – this should be very slightly higher, to ensure a slight fall to the front, so that the steps shed rainwater.

Then fill with concrete: a fairly stiff rather than very wet or runny mix, which could run down over the stones or bricks and spoil them. Leave a rough finish, as a very smooth surface will be slippery in wet weather.

When the concrete has hardened repeat the procedure for further steps. The subsequent risers should be set on the rear edges of the preceding treads.

Slab and brick steps

These are also quite easy to build (see Fig. 19). Lay the slabs on well-rammed hardcore. The first or lowest step should have a concrete foundation 10 cm (4 in) thick. The first riser should be set on this: one or two courses of bricks which should be bonded with mortar. Fill in behind this first riser with hardcore, well consolidated, to the level of the riser. Then lay paving slabs to form the first tread. Bed the slabs on mortar. You will need to spread a layer of mortar over the brick riser as well. The slabs should overhang the risers by at least 2.5 cm (1 in) as this gives a more pleasing appearance.

The second riser is built on the rear edge of the first tread. Continue building up in this way until the flight is completed.

Log steps

These are the simplest steps to build, as shown in Fig. 20, and are especially recommended for natural or woodland gardens. The logs are held in place with stout wooden stakes driven well into the ground. The stakes should be treated with horticultural wood preservative.

Well-rammed soil forms the treads. To make this more stable and quite hard, you can mix dry cement into the surface before firming it. The cement will harden and bind the soil. Alternatively treads could be surfaced with pulverized bark to overcome muddy conditions.

Opposite: *Here again, the trick of making paths disappear from view has been cleverly utilized. This garden is so well planted that virtually every part is a secret area.*

Fig. 17. *Laying a concrete path. A 10 cm (4 in) layer of well-rammed hardcore (a) makes a good foundation. Erect timber shuttering along the proposed edges (b), the top of which indicates the level of the concrete. The concrete can be laid 8 cm (3 in) thick and should be tamped well down with a wooden plank on edge (c). When the concrete has partially set, create the final surface, which may be smooth if a trowel is used (d) or textured if lightly brushed with a stiff broom (e).*

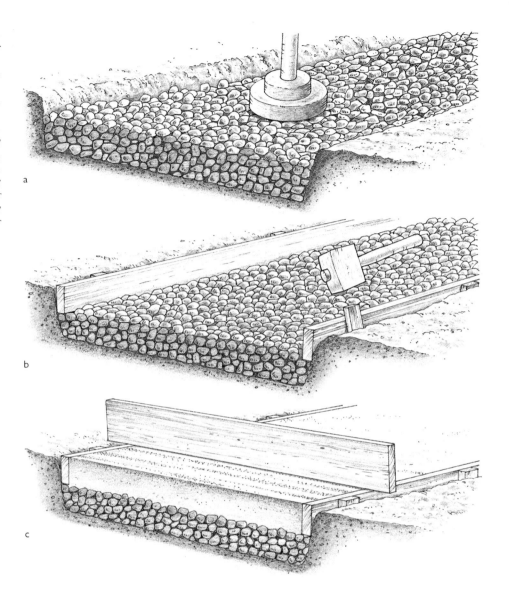

POOLS, FOUNTAINS AND WATERFALLS

Water features are very easily constructed today if use is made of modern materials and equipment.

Pools

A pool, whether formal or informal, is constructed with marginal shelves, about 23 cm (9 in) deep (below water level) and 23 cm wide, to hold baskets of marginal aquatic plants. Pool depth is important, too: the central portion of a small pool should be 45 cm (18 in) deep and preferably deeper. For large pools the depth can be up to 90 cm (3 ft).

The easiest way to construct a pool is to use one of the modern pool liners. These allow you to make a pool, or even a stream, of any shape and size.

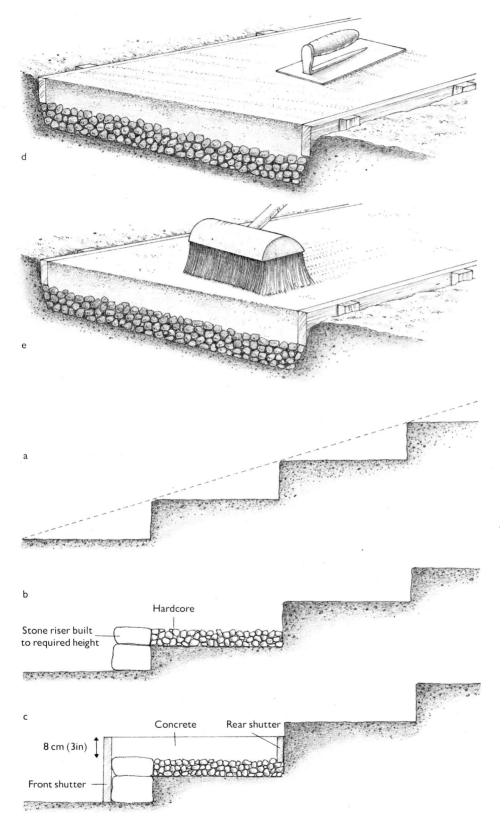

d

e

a

b

Stone riser built
to required height

Hardcore

c

Concrete   Rear shutter

8 cm (3in)

Front shutter

Fig. 18. *Building concrete steps. Start by roughly excavating the shape of the steps in the bank (a). Lay first riser (b), using building blocks or bricks. Cover tread area behind with hardcore and firm it well. Then install wooden shuttering across front of riser and also at the back of the tread (c). Fill with a stiff concrete mix to a depth of 8 cm (3 in).*

Fig. 19. *Slab and brick steps are easy to build, laying the slabs on well-rammed hardcore. The slabs should overhang the risers by at least 2.5 cm (1 in) as this gives a more pleasing appearance.*

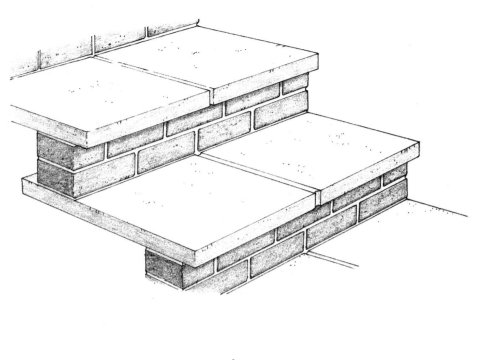

Fig. 20. *Log steps are the simplest to built and are especially recommended for natural or woodland gardens. The wooden stakes should be well driven into the ground. Well-rammed soil forms the treads.*

The cheapest pool liner is 500 gauge black polythene, but it has a short life and does not stretch, so it does not mould very well to the shape of the pool. Therefore I do not recommend this for a permanent water feature.

In the medium price range are PVC liners which have a much longer life; they stretch and mould to the shape of the pool and are reparable. They come in various pastel colours and some are reinforced with Terylene webbing.

The most expensive liner is butyl rubber which has an extremely long life and is highly recommended for permanent water features. It is matt

Steps are always enticing and should be used wherever possible as entrances to secret areas. This flight takes one to a secluded patio, surrounded with luxuriant foliage.

black, readily stretches and moulds itself to the shape of the pool and is reparable.

To calculate the size of liner required (PVC or butyl rubber), use the following formula: maximum length of pool plus twice maximum depth times maximum width plus twice maximum depth. This takes into account marginal shelves and a generous overlap at the top.

For a pool of irregular shape, base the calculations on a rectangle which encloses the greatest width and length of the pool.

The basic steps in pool construction, using a liner, are as follows.

- With a length of hosepipe or rope define the shape of the pool on a pre-levelled side.
- Excavate, leaving marginal shelves, and slope the sides 20 degrees inwards for stability (Fig. 21).
- The top edge of the pool must be perfectly level so insert short pegs all round, at 90 cm (3 ft) intervals and get the tops level with a spirit level. The ground must be level with all the pegs.
- Check the excavation for stones as these could puncture the liner. Line with moist soft sand about 2.5 cm (1 in) thick to buffer the liner against stones, roots etc. If you find it easier, the sides can be lined with thick layers of wet newspaper.
- Remove levelling pegs and lay the liner loosely in the excavation with an even overlap all round the edge. Place bricks or paving slabs on the overlap to anchor the liner.
- Start filling the pool with water. As the pool fills gradually ease off all the

Fig. 21. *Basic steps in pool construction, using a liner. The excavation, with marginal shelves (a). The bottom and shelves can be lined with soft sand, and the sides with thick layers of wet newspaper. Lay liner loosely in the excavation with ample overlap all round and fill with water (b). Edge the pool, covering the overlap, with paving slabs or natural flat stone (c).*

bricks or slabs. You will find that the liner then moulds to the shape of the pool.
- If necessary cut off surplus liner, but leave an overlap of 15–20 cm (6–8 in).
- Edge the pool, covering the overlap, with paving slabs or natural flat stone, bedding them on mortar. They should overlap the edge of the pool by 5 cm (2 in) or so, so that the liner is completely hidden.

A raised pool is built up with bricks or ornamental concrete walling blocks. Marginal shelves can be built with bricks. Smooth off the mortar well on the inside as if left rough it could puncture the liner. Insert liner as described above. Then top off with coping stones, which hide the overlap of the liner. Bed them on mortar.

Bog garden

A bog garden is often created next to a sunken pool and can be made water-retentive by means of the pool liner. Buy a liner longer than is needed for the actual pool. Take out an excavation about 30 cm (12 in) deep for the bog garden and run the extra length of pool liner into it. Above the liner separate the pool and the bog area with a retaining wall of stones or bricks loosely laid.

Once the liner is in place put a layer of gravel in the bottom of the bog garden and then fill up with peaty soil: which should be at least 2.5 cm (1 in) above the level of the pool. The pool water will then seep through the retaining wall, keeping the bog garden moist.

Pumps

If you are to have a waterfall or fountain then you will need a suitable electric pump.

Fig. 22. *A simple fountain can consist of a jet unit on the outlet of a submersible pump. The jets are interchangeable for different patterns.*

Submersible pumps are popular. The pump is stood on the bottom of the pool on a level plinth. It expels water through a fountain jet (which must be just above water level), or through a length of hosepipe to serve a waterfall. Some pumps have outlets for both fountain and waterfall. The pump is connected to the mains electricity supply using thick waterproof cable and waterproof cable connector.

You should obtain advice from an expert before installing an electricity supply.

The pump should be placed near to the base of a waterfall. It should be removed and stored for the winter.

The pump must be powerful enough for your waterfall, so calculate the rate of flow needed for your particular feature, as follows:

1   Place a hosepipe at the top of the waterfall and connect it to a tap. Turn on the water until you have a good flow and complete cover.

2   Collect the water for a period of one minute.

3   Measure the amount collected in pints, multiply by 7.5 and the result is the number of gallons the pump will need to be capable of raising every hour for a satisfactory flow.

The alternative to the submersible pump is the surface pump. This is recommended for large features—for example, a very high waterfall or several fountains. It needs housing in a brick-built chamber at the side of the pool (as near as possible to the fountain and/or waterfall), and it can be above or below the level of the pool water. Water is drawn from the pool via a pipe fitted with a filter, but full details on installation should be obtained from the supplier.

A surface pump is cheaper than the equivalent submersible, but is noisier, and of course you have the cost of building the chamber.

Fountains

A simple fountain (Fig. 22) consists of a jet unit on the outlet of a submersible pump, or on some figure or ornament linked to a surface pump. The jets are interchangeable for different patterns.

It is possible to buy more complex fountains with various spray patterns—even illuminated for night-time use.

An impressive fountain consists of a series of bowls mounted on a central stem, the lower bowls having increasingly larger diameters. Water is pumped up the central stem to the top bowl, and flows down from one to the other, then back into the pool.

A bubble fountain (Fig. 23) has a waterproof concrete sump below ground level which is kept filled with water and houses a submersible pump. Over the top is placed a strong steel grid. On top is placed an old millstone with a central hole—or, more often, a concrete imitation. Around the millstone is placed a layer of large ornamental pebbles. Water is pumped, via a

Fig. 23. A bubble fountain has water bubbling through the central hole of an old millstone – or at least a concrete imitation – and makes an attractive feature for a patio, for instance.

Fig. 24. A simple waterfall, using a submersible pump and a length of hosepipe to the head. It consists of a series of rocks set like a flight of steps. A row of rocks should also be placed down each side to guide the water and prevent it flowing over the edges.

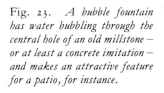

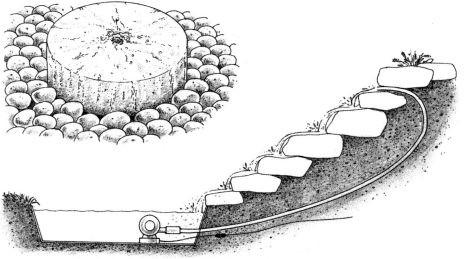

Taking steps to the extreme maybe? Nevertheless they make one want to explore – provided one has the energy!

hose, up through the central hole of the millstone and bubbles out at the top, flowing over the stone and back down to the sump through the pebbles.

Waterfalls

A simple waterfall, using a submersible pump and a length of hosepipe to the head, is shown in Fig. 24. It consists of a series of rocks set like a flight of steps. A row of rocks should also be placed down each side, to guide the water and prevent it flowing over the edges. It should be noted that the pump is set on a level plinth.

ROCK GARDENS

Before attempting to build a rock garden, eradicate all perennial weeds by treating them when in full growth with a weedkiller containing glyphosate, as once a rock garden is built they are very difficult to control.

If the rock garden is to be built into a bank soil drainage should not be a problem. However, if it is to be built on a flat site make sure drainage is really good. On poorly drained soils it pays to excavate 30 cm (12 in) of the topsoil and replace with 15 cm (6 in) of rubble topped with a 30 cm (12 in) layer of compost, which can consist of 7 parts loam, 3 parts peat and 2 parts coarse sand or grit (parts by volume). If the soil is well drained all you need do is dig it to the depth of your spade and incorporate grit and peat.

Whether building on a bank or on the flat, form the ground into the required contours or shapes and then thoroughly firm it.

Try to use large pieces of rock, not lots of small bits. The maximum weight that one person can comfortably handle is 25 kg ($\frac{1}{2}$ cwt).

The best 'face' of each rock should face forwards and the strata lines should all run in the same direction (usually horizontally).

Whatever type of rock garden you are building, always start with a 'keystone' for each outcrop you are constructing. This is a large, well-shaped piece of rock, from which you work. Further rocks are placed on each side of the keystone and should appear to be part of it. Aim to give the impression that each outcrop is one large piece of rock.

Cut out a bed for each rock—no more than a quarter of each rock need be buried. Ram the soil well behind the rocks as they must be really firm.

When building a rock garden on a bank aim to create a series of natural-looking terraces with flat beds between them for planting. The rocks should tilt slightly into the bank, as shown in Fig. 25. If desired, bold cliffs can be constructed as shown in Fig. 26. Place hard stones between rocks to keep them apart and fill the joints with compost. (Later, alpines can be planted in these joints.)

The beds can be prepared for planting by adding peat and grit to the soil. Or if the soil is very heavy and sticky replace it with compost as described above.

Fig. 25. *The construction of a rock garden on a bank. Aim to create a series of natural-looking terraces, with flat beds between them for planting. The rocks should tilt slightly into the bank.*

Fig. 26. *Bold cliffs can be constructed by stacking rocks one on top of the other. Spaces can be left between them, filled with soil in which plants can be grown.*

Fig. 27. *A flat rock garden consists of a number of low outcrops of rock with planting spaces or beds between them.*

A flat rock garden can consist of a number of low outcrops as shown in Fig. 27, with planting spaces or beds between them.

Building a grotto

First you excavate a hole in the base of the bank – ideally a semi-circular hole. The walls can be lined with rocks, building up with rectangular pieces. They could be bonded with mortar for extra strength.

Next you will need to install the 'roof'. One way of doing this is to lay a large flat thick piece of rock over the excavation. Bear in mind, though, that this would be extremely heavy and several people would be needed to move it and lever it into place. It should be bedded on to rocks firmly placed on each side of the excavation, and at the back, too. The piece of rock should substantially overlap the walls of the grotto.

You might find it easier to form the roof from timber railway sleepers. The problem here is that the front edge will need to be disguised. But you could grow trailing plants or ferns over it. The roof of a grotto should be higher at the front than at the back so that you can easily see inside.

The top of the grotto can then be covered with soil and rocks – in other words, integrating it into the rest of the rock garden.

A final word of advice. Don't be too adventurous and make a large grotto, as there would be too many problems involved in building it—especially the roof. Instead be content with a smallish feature which is much easier to construct.

SUNKEN GARDEN

If you do not have a natural hollow in your garden then make an excavation of the shape desired—usually square or rectangular, but you may decide on a circular one.

The retaining walls are usually about 60 cm (2 ft) high and can be two bricks in thickness. Use either bricks or ornamental concrete walling blocks of about brick size. For details of building, see the section on Walls (p.85). It is advisable to top them with coping. Do not forget to leave drainage holes at regular intervals along the base of the walls; insert lengths of earthenware drain pipe through the wall, placing some rubble behind them.

TERRACES

A garden in the truly English style, with paths leading in all directions – a garden full of surprises.

When building a raised terrace against the house there is a very important point to bear in mind—the surface of the terrace must be at least 5 cm (2 in)

below the damp-proof course. If you are unable to locate the DPC then seek professional advice, for if you build above it you will be risking rising damp in the house walls.

You will need to build a substantial three-sided retaining wall and I would advise not going too high otherwise construction becomes more complex and, besides, if you have a smallish garden it may look out of pro-portion. I would, therefore, suggest a terrace of between 60 and 90 cm (2 and 3 ft) in height.

The walls are best built of bricks on a substantial foundation, as described in the section on Walls (p.85). They should be two or, ideally, three bricks thick. Don't forget to include drainage holes along the bottom (e.g. sections of earthenware pipe) to ensure any rainwater is able to escape.

If you do decide to build above 90 cm (3 ft) then the walls should have steel reinforcing rods through them, the rods being bedded in the concrete foundations.

Inside the retaining walls the soil should be well consolidated and foundations laid as described in the section on Paving (p.93). Then paving slabs are laid, ensuring they slightly overlap the edges of the walls—say by about 2.5 cm (1 in).

Bear in mind during construction that the terrace should slope slightly away from the house so that rainwater readily runs off.

In a large garden a stone balustrade around the terrace is very attractive

An excellent example of a formal pool, well planted with waterlilies and with the white arum or zantedeschia. Statuary adds to the romantic atmosphere.

but it looks a bit pompous in a small garden. In this instance the terrace would be better with a low parapet wall around the edge, say about 45 cm (18 in) high.

PERGOLAS

There are various ways of building a pergola and the structure can be straight—for example, spanning a path—or it can be L-shaped, maybe for partly covering a patio.

The pillars or uprights should be 2.4 m (8 ft) high and spaced 1.8–2.4 m (6–8 ft) apart.

A traditional brick and timber pergola is attractive, especially in a cottage or country garden. It is quite a bulky structure, so make sure you have plenty of space to set it off.

First, you build up brick pillars, each on a firm foundation of hardcore and concrete. Each pillar should have two steel reinforcing rods through the centre, bedded into the concrete foundation. Four bricks are laid for each course to form a square pillar—it will be about 33 cm (13 in) square. Make sure the reinforcing rods are enveloped in mortar as you build.

The pillars support a grid framework of sawn boards 15 by 5 cm (6 by 2 in), slotted together. The boards are used on edge. The timber should be treated with a horticultural wood preservative.

All-timber pergolas are popular and can be bought in kit form ready for assembly. Or you may prefer to make your own. The timber uprights should be sunk at least 60 cm (2 ft) into the ground, and ideally concreted in. All timber can be 10 by 5 cm (4 by 2 in) with a sawn finish. The uprights are joined together in pairs and further timbers are then used lengthways to form a grid framework. A similar pergola can be constructed of peeled larch poles if you want a very rustic effect. The poles are joined together by notching and nailing them.

SUPPORTS FOR CLIMBERS

To support climbing plants on walls and fences you could secure heavy gauge wires, about 30 cm (12 in) apart, to the wall or fence. Use either galvanized or plastic-coated wire. They can be supported with vine eyes, available for timber or masonry. If you want really tight wires then use a straining bolt at one end of each.

Alternatively trellis panels could be fixed to the wall or fence, using suitable brackets. The panels should be set about 5 cm (2 in) away from the wall to allow good air circulation behind the plants. Trellis panels are available in wood, plastic-coated steel and strong plastic. Wooden trellis will need to be treated regularly with a horticultural timber preservative.

GARDEN ROOMS AND CONSERVATORIES

A garden room or conservatory must be built on an adequate base and comply with building regulations. Many structures will need a concrete slab 10 cm (4 in) thick overall laid on at least 10 cm (4 in) of hardcore. The concrete is thickened at the edges to a depth of at least 30 cm (12 in). Then a damp-proof membrane is laid over this followed by a cement and sand screed 5 cm (2 in) deep.

Some conservatory manufacturers, especially those who supply lean-to greenhouses, provide a prefabricated base which could simply be positioned on concrete footings of a suitable depth, again laid on hardcore. The company who supplies the conservatory will advise on a suitable base and your local authority will advise on building regulations.

One has the choice of building the base oneself or employing a local builder. It is likely that the base, and maybe the completed structure, will be examined by your local building inspector.

Some conservatory companies undertake site erection and glazing while others may recommend an erection service. A local builder should also be able to erect a conservatory for you, following the manufacturer's instructions.

Alternatively you may prefer to put up the conservatory yourself. Some are easier to assemble than others. The modular conservatories, which come in sections, are straightforward; more difficult and time-consuming are the metal-framed conservatories and lean-to greenhouses. These are supplied in kit form and there are many parts to assemble. But step-by-step instructions are supplied and should be closely followed. It is a good idea to study the instructions thoroughly before making a start.

Timber-framed lean-to greenhouses and conservatories are easy to put up as they are supplied in sections which are simply bolted together.

Putting up a conservatory is much easier if two people are involved and for larger structures it is essential to have two pairs of hands.

PLANTING

This is what the professionals call 'soft landscaping'. To ensure plants establish quickly it is important to prepare the site well, to use the correct planting technique and to plant at the right time of year. Here I will consider the planting of all the major groups of plants that have been covered in previous chapters.

CLEARING THE GROUND

Before creating any feature the ground must be completely cleared of perennial weeds like couch grass, brambles, nettles, bindweed, ground elder and docks. During the growing season—spring and summer—the weeds should be sprayed with a suitable weedkiller, used according to the manufacturer's instructions. For broad-leaved weeds such as ground elder and brambles use a weedkiller containing glyphosate. For perennial grasses, like couch grass, use a weedkiller containing alloxydim sodium. If used correctly the weeds should be dead by the autumn, when digging can commence.

DIGGING

Proposed planting sites should ideally be dug to two depths of the spade (double digging), especially if the land has been neglected or if the soil is poorly drained. Double digging helps to improve drainage and breaks up any hard layers of soil below the surface, encouraging plants to root deeply.

During digging bulky organic matter should be added to each trench. This improves all soils, whether light sandy or chalky types or heavy clays. It not only helps to improve drainage of heavy soils but also assists in conserving moisture in naturally well-drained types.

Suitable organic matter is well-rotted farmyard manure, garden compost, spent hops, spent mushroom compost, pulverized bark and peat. Spread a layer over the bottom of each trench—as a guide, a quarter of a barrowload will be adequate for each 1.2 m (4 ft) length of trench. If you have a very dry soil it is advisable to mix organic matter into the top 30 cm (12 in) as well. Badly drained soil would benefit also from the addition of grit or coarse sand during digging. Again place it in each trench and mix plenty into the topsoil.

Before planting, the roughly dug soil should be broken down with a fork and well firmed by treading. Work into the surface a base dressing of general-purpose fertilizer.

SHRUBS AND CONIFERS

Evergreen shrubs and conifers which are supplied root-balled (that is, lifted from the nurseryman's field, with a ball of soil around the roots which is tightly wrapped with hessian) are planted in early to mid-autumn or mid- to late spring. At these periods the soil is warm and so the young plants quickly become established. Containerized evergreen shrubs and conifers are planted in spring, summer or early autumn, for the same reason. By containerized I mean plants grown in plastic pots or flexible polythene bags, as supplied by garden centres.

Deciduous shrubs which are supplied bare-rooted (as lifted from the field) are planted between late autumn and early spring, while they are dormant. Containerized deciduous shrubs can be planted at any time of the year provided the ground is not very wet or frozen.

To plant a root-balled or containerized shrub or conifer, first take out a hole slightly larger than the root-ball and of such a depth that after planting the top of the root-ball is only slightly below soil level. Ensure the root-ball is thoroughly moist before planting, then carefully remove the container or hessian wrap. Place the plant in the centre of the hole and return fine soil around it, at the same time firming well by treading with your heels.

With bare-root shrubs take out a hole sufficiently large to allow the roots to be spread out to their full extent—they should not turn upwards at the ends. Plant to the same depth that the shrub was growing in the field—this is indicated by a soil mark at the base of the stems. Trim back any broken or damaged roots, then place the plant in the centre of the hole. Return some fine soil over the roots and then gently shake the plant up and down to work this soil well between the roots. Return the rest of the soil, and as you do so firm it thoroughly by treading with your heels.

If your soil is poor it is a good idea to use a proprietary planting mixture, which consists of peat with fertilizers added. Work some of this into the bottom of the planting hole and into the soil which is to be returned around the plant. This gets plants off to a good start.

Newly planted shrubs and conifers must be kept watered if the soil starts to dry out. This should be continued until they are fully established.

When planting shrubs in groups sufficient space should be left between them for full development. Spacing varies according to the spread of the plants, but a useful guide is to allow a distance which equals at least two-thirds of their ultimate height.

Steps entice one to this raised, intimate patio which is well planted with summer flowers and shrubs. Note the trellis-work, which provides support for climbers.

CLIMBERS

The principles of planting shrubs apply equally to climbers. An additional point to bear in mind is that climbers must not be planted hard up against a wall or fence, where the soil can be very dry and inhibit establishment. Instead plant about 30 cm (12 in) away from the wall or fence, and guide the stems to their supports by means of bamboo canes angled in towards the wall or fence. On average, climbers are spaced 2.4–3.6 m (8–12 ft) apart along a wall or fence.

TREES

Once again, follow the planting advice given under shrubs. A major addition, though, is to provide a stake for support for the first year or two, until the tree has rooted sufficiently into the soil to support itself adequately.

Use an 8 cm (3 in) stake and insert it in the planting hole before the tree is positioned. It should be slightly off-centre of the hole. The stake should be sufficiently long to allow it to be inserted 45–60 cm (18–24 in) into the ground, with the top only just below the lowest branch of the tree. After planting secure the trunk to the stake with plastic buckle-type tree ties: one at the top, another about 30 cm (12 in) above ground level, and a third mid-way between the two. They should be tight, ensuring there is a rubber or plastic buffer between the stake and trunk.

A containerized tree often has a large root-ball so you cannot get the stake close to the trunk. In this instance, insert two stakes a suitable distance apart and then nail a cross piece of timber at the top. Tie the tree to this cross piece, again using a plastic buckle-type tree tie.

Tree ties should be inspected every six months and if they are becoming very tight slacken them off.

If you are planting several trees remember that small ornamental kinds will need to be spaced 7.5–9 m (25–30 ft) apart each way, while large forest-type trees will need considerably more space (indeed they are usually planted as single, isolated specimens).

HEDGES AND SCREENS

Before planting a hedge or screen prepare a 1–1.2 m (3–4 ft) wide strip by double digging and adding bulky organic matter. For timing and techniques of planting evergreen and deciduous subjects see Shrubs, above.

A single line of plants is normal, but if you want a really wide hedge plant in a double staggered row.

Planting distances are important. Below are the distances for those hedging plants recommended in Chapter 3.

Formal hedges
The following subjects are planted 30 cm (12 in) apart: *Ligustrum ovalifolium*, *Lonicera nitida*.

Plant at 45 cm (18 in) apart: *Buxus sempervirens*, *Carpinus betulus*, *Euonymus japonicus*, *Fagus sylvatica*, *Ilex aquifolium*, *Taxus baccata*.

Needing 60 cm (24 in) spacing are: *Chamaecyparis lawsoniana*, × *Cupressocyparis leylandii*, *Cupressus macrocarpa*, *Prunus laurocerasus*, *Prunus lusitanica*, *Thuja occidentalis*, *Thuja plicata*.

Informal hedges
Plant at 30 cm (12 in) apart: *Pyracantha atalantioides*.

The following are planted 45 cm (18 in) apart: *Berberis darwinii*, *Berberis* × *stenophylla*, *Cotoneaster lacteus*, *Viburnum tinus*.

Needing 60 cm (24 in) spacing are *Elaeagnus pungens* 'Maculata', *Escallonia rubra macrantha*, *Rhododendron ponticum*.

Tall screens
When used as tall screens, *Chamaecyparis lawsoniana*, × *Cupressocyparis leylandii*, *Cupressus macrocarpa* and *Thuja plicata* are planted 1.8–2.4 m (6–8 ft) apart in a single row; or they could be planted in a double staggered row to make a very wide screen.

ROSES

Planting times and techniques are as for deciduous shrubs.

Recommended planting distances are: large-flowered (hybrid tea) and cluster-flowered (floribunda) varieties, 60 cm (2 ft) apart each way; shrub roses, 1.8–2.4 m (6–8 ft); miniatures, 30 cm (12 in); climbers and ramblers, 2.4 m (8 ft); and ground-cover roses, 60–120 cm (2–4 ft) apart each way depending on vigour. An additional point to bear in mind when planting roses is that the budding union (the swollen part at the base of the stem) should be just below soil level.

PERENNIALS

Hardy border perennials and similar plants such as herbs can be planted in early or mid-spring as then they establish quickly because the soil is warming up and becoming drier. Autumn planting can only be safely done if the soil is very well drained.

Container-grown plants should be planted in a hole only slightly larger than the root-ball. Bare-root plants and your own divisions should have planting holes which are deep enough to allow the roots to dangle straight down to their full length. In both cases the crown of the plant (that is, where the dormant buds are situated) should be level with the surrounding soil after planting: the buds should not be covered with soil.

LAWNS

Lawns can be created from seed or turf. Grass seed is supplied in mixtures of various kinds of grasses for different purposes. If you want a fine ornamental lawn choose a mixture which contains fine-leaved grasses such as fescues and bents. Such a lawn needs a lot of maintenance.

If a lawn is to have a great deal of use choose a utility mixture which contains hardwearing grasses like perennial ryegrass and meadow grasses. These have broader leaves than fescues and bents.

There are grass-seed mixtures suitable for shady sites and these include such species as fine-leaved fescue and rough-stalked meadow grass.

The best periods for sowing grass seed are spring and early autumn. Sow at the rate of 30–60 g per square metre (1–2 oz per square yard).

Turves should be bought from a specialist supplier – you will have a choice of turves for different purposes as discussed above. There is a choice of field-grown turf, which is usually supplied in 90 by 30 cm (3 by 1 ft) pieces; or seedling turf which is supplied in large lightweight rolls.

Field-grown turf is laid in autumn, winter or early spring; seedling turf should not be laid in winter. No turfing should be undertaken in summer as conditions can be too dry. Field-grown turves are laid staggered like bricks in a wall, while rolls of seedling turf are laid in strips.

PREPARING CONTAINERS FOR PLANTING

Ornamental containers (tubs, pots, urns etc.) which are to be used for plants must have drainage holes in the bottom. These should be covered with a

Planted paving, featuring such plants as red valerian, helianthemums and alchemilla, leading to a sitting area under an arbour.

layer of drainage material, such as 'crocks' or broken clay flower pots. First put a large piece over each hole, then a layer of smaller pieces. Cover the crocks with a layer of rough peat or leafmould, then fill with a suitable compost.

For permanent plants a soil-based potting compost is best, such as John Innes potting compost No. 2. Use an ericaceous mix, though, for lime-hating plants. Proprietary mixtures are generally peat-based. Short-term plants, such as spring and summer bedding, can either be grown in John Innes potting compost No. 2 or in peat-based (soilless) potting compost.

A delightful little patio surrounded with plantings of peonies, marguerites, roses and other flowers of summer (garden designers: Hillier & Hilton).

AQUATICS

Aquatics such as marginal plants and waterlilies are planted in plastic aquatic baskets. First line the basket with hessian, then insert the plant, using a medium or heavy fibrous loam. Leave space at the top and cover the loam with a layer of pea shingle to prevent it being washed away. Baskets 30 cm (12 in) square are suitable for the more vigorous plants; while 20 cm (8 in) square baskets are best for those of restrained habit, including miniature waterlilies. Planting time is mid- to late spring.

7
CARE AND MAINTENANCE

Many garden features need proper and regular maintenance to keep them looking good and to ensure a long life. Plants should also be cared for correctly—pruned if necessary, fed and watered and kept free from weeds.

———— GARDEN HARDWARE ————

BRICKWORK

To prevent frost and moisture penetrating walls the mortar bonding must be replaced if it starts to crumble. Chisel it out to a depth of about 12 mm ($\frac{1}{2}$ in) and refill with mortar, using a builder's trowel, and pressing it into a V shape. Check coping as well: if this has badly deteriorated replace it.

If a garden wall is to be painted for decorative effect, use an exterior cement-based masonry paint (those containing fine sand are particularly long-lasting). Old flaking or loose paint should first be removed.

Green algae and moss can build up on walls, rendering them unsightly. Treat walls with a commercial algicide, particularly if you intend to paint them. This will kill the algae and moss, which can then be scraped off.

ORNAMENTAL WROUGHT IRONWORK

Wrought-iron gates, railings etc., should be regularly painted to prevent them from rusting. Either use an undercoat plus exterior-grade gloss paint; or a paint with a hammered enamel finish. Only one coat is needed of the latter and it can be applied direct to rusty surfaces, after rubbing off the loose rust.

TIMBER

Fences, trelliswork, pergolas and summerhouses should be regularly treated with a horticultural timber preservative, or painted if preferred, to prevent moisture entering the timber and causing it to rot. Treatment every two or three years may be needed, depending on the local climate and weather conditions.

Use a modern horticultural timber preservative as this will not harm plants, such as the water-based type which contains furmecyclox, available in red cedar, dark oak and golden chestnut.

You may want to paint some features, such as ranch-type fencing and conservatories. Rub down old paintwork well to remove any flaking paint. Prime any bare wood, then apply an undercoat followed by a top coat of exterior-grade gloss paint. Alternatively consider using the new micro-porous paint, which is applied to bare wood, needing no primer or undercoat.

PAVED AREAS

Weeds can grow in paved areas—they appear in the joints between slabs or bricks, especially if these are not filled with mortar. Weeds certainly establish in gravel areas. You can control them by spraying the area with a proprietary path weedkiller, provided it does not come in contact with cultivated plants (follow manufacturer's instructions). Alternatively you could spot treat weeds with paraquat or glyphosate, but again do not allow these to come in contact with cultivated plants.

POOLS

Water in a new pool will turn green—like pea soup. On no account change the water but allow it to clear naturally. This it will do if the pool is well planted with oxygenating plants. Blanket weed (masses of thin thread-like green growths) should be pulled out with a garden rake—if left, it will take over the pool.

Top up the pool with fresh water during the summer as necessary, as water is lost through evaporation.

GARDEN ROOMS OR CONSERVATORIES

Apart from timber preservation or painting, as described above, the glass must be kept scrupulously clean to allow maximum light transmission. There are horticultural glass cleaners available which remove green algae and grime, leaving the glass sparkling. If applicable, overlaps between panes of glass can be cleaned out by inserting a thin plastic plant label between them.

PLANTS

WEED CONTROL

If perennial weeds were eradicated before planting you should only have annual weeds to control. But this is no small problem, for they can quickly form a thick carpet around plants which can seriously retard growth, so they must be kept in check.

Of course, there is the traditional hoeing, which should be done regularly, while weeds are in the seedling stage, choosing a warm dry day when the soil surface is dry. But this is time-consuming and you may find it more convenient to use a weedkiller.

Provided it does not come in contact with cultivated plants, paraquat can be used among shrubs, roses etc, quickly killing off annual weeds. To prevent weed seeds from germinating, simazine can be applied to weed-free soil around plants and the effect lasts for many months. Alternatively, use propachlor granules which prevent weed germination for up to eight weeks. After applying these weedkillers the soil surface must not be disturbed.

Odd perennial weeds can be 'spot-treated' with a weedkiller containing glyphosate, but keep it off cultivated plants.

MULCHING

This technique is highly recommended, for not only does it suppress annual weeds but also helps to conserve soil moisture during dry weather. It makes for a labour-saving garden as well as benefitting the plants.

A mulch is a 5–8 cm (2–3 in) layer of bulky organic matter placed over the soil surface around and among plants. Suitable materials include well-rotted farmyard manure, garden compost, peat, leafmould, spent mushroom compost, spent hops and pulverized bark. The latter lasts the longest. Peat, leafmould and bark are probably the most attractive-looking mulching materials. They are certainly recommended for woodland areas and shrub beds.

Apply a mulch only to moist weed-free soil and top up as necessary in the spring.

A mineral mulch of pea shingle about 2.5 cm (1 in) deep can be used in certain parts of the garden, such as the rock garden, and maybe beds in and around a patio, especially if they contain permanent plants.

FEEDING

All plants should be fed regularly to keep them growing well. Permanent plants can be given a topdressing of general-purpose fertilizer, such as Growmore, in the spring. Roses and other flowering shrubs could be fed with a proprietary rose fertilizer.

Blood, fish and bone fertilizer is good for all but lime-hating plants and provides all the major plant foods. For temporary plants, such as spring and summer bedding, apply a base dressing to the soil before planting, using a general-purpose fertilizer.

Now let us take a look at some specific requirements of the various groups of plants which have been discussed in previous chapters.

SHRUBS

Some shrubs need regular pruning and for this purpose they can be placed into various groups, as follows.

A. Deciduous shrubs flowering on shoots which were formed in the previous growing season. Various spring- and early summer-flowering shrubs are in this group, including such popular ones as *Ribes sanguineum*, forsythia, *Kerria japonica*, spiraeas like *S. × arguta* and *S. thunbergii*, deutzia, philadelphus and weigela. As soon as flowering is over, stems or branches that carried the flowers should be cut back to young shoots which are growing lower down. In the following year these shoots will bear the flowers. Also, remove completely about one-quarter of the oldest stems.

B. This group embraces deciduous shrubs which flower on current year's shoots. They are pruned hard in late winter/early spring, resulting in vigorous shoots which produce flowers in summer or early autumn. Some shrubs have all their stems cut down to ground level. With others we allow a framework of woody branches to develop to the desired height, usually

Here one emerges from a tunnel of foliage into a sunken garden, with scented philadelphus or mock orange to greet the visitor.

60–90 cm (2–3 ft), and then prune shoots close to this framework (leaving one or two buds on each). Examples of popular shrubs in this group include: *Buddleia davidii* (allow a woody framework); ceanothus (allow a woody framework); and hardy fuchsias (cut to ground level).

C. This group contains deciduous shrubs which are grown for their coloured bark, like *Cornus alba* and varieties, *Cornus stolonifera* 'Flaviramea' and *Salix alba* 'Chermesina'. They are pruned in early spring. Allow a woody framework to build up to the desired height (usually a couple of feet or so) and prune shoots hard back to this framework, to within one or two buds of their base.

D. This group contains deciduous and evergreen shrubs that should have dead flower heads removed immediately after flowering. This is to prevent seed production, so encouraging stronger vegetative growth, and for the sake of appearance. Popular shrubs in this group are cytisus (remove tops of shoots containing seed pods but don't cut into older wood); callunas and ericas (heathers)–trim plants lightly with shears to remove dead flowers but don't cut into old wood; lavender (use shears to remove dead flowers); lilac or syringa (use secateurs to remove dead flowers but avoid new buds below); rhodondendrons (twist off dead blooms but watch out for new buds below); and *Potentilla fruticosa* varieties (after flowering trim lightly with shears).

CLIMBERS

There are several climbing plants which need regular pruning.

Clematis. These popular climbers are grouped according to method of pruning.

A. Hybrids and species which bloom in summer and autumn on new shoots produced in the current growing season, such as *C.* × *jackmanii, C. orientalis, C. tangutica, C. viticella*, 'Hagley Hybrid', 'Ernest Markham' and 'Perle d'Azur'. All of the previous year's growth is cut back almost to ground level during late winter. Make the cuts just above strong growth buds.

B. In the main there are vigorous species which flower in the early spring on short shoots from growth produced during the previous summer. *Clematis montana* and its varieties are in this group, together with *C. macropetala* and *C alpina. C. montana*, a very vigorous clematis, should ideally be allotted sufficient space and left unpruned. Prune others as follows: cut out all flowered wood to within a few centimetres of the main framework immediately flowering is over – spring or early summer.

C. In this group are all the large-flowered hybrids which bloom from late spring to midsummer on shoots formed in the previous year. Well-known examples are 'Nelly Moser', 'Henryi', 'Lasurstern', 'The President' and 'Vyvyan Pennell'. There are two pruning options: you can leave them unpruned, or only lightly prune them, but when they become out of control or straggly they can be cut back in late winter, to within 90 cm (3 ft) of the ground. Or you can treat these clematis like those in group A: in late winter cut them back virtually to ground level; flowering will then be in late summer.

Hedera (ivies)   In early spring prune side shoots hard back – almost to the main stems. This will remove most of the foliage, the idea being to reduce weight. However the plants will soon produce plenty of new foliage.

Jasminum nudiflorum   The popular winter jasmine is pruned immediately after flowering by cutting back the old side shoots which carried flowers almost to the main framework of stems.

Jasminum officinale   This is the equally popular summer jasmine, which is pruned in late winter by removing completely some of the oldest stems to prevent a tangled mass of growth.

Lonicera periclymenum varieties   The honeysuckles can be pruned in late winter by reducing some of the oldest stems by half to two-thirds.

Vitis vinifera 'Brandt'   This popular grape vine is pruned in winter while it is dormant, by cutting back all the side shoots produced on the main stems to within one or two buds.

Wisteria   In midsummer cut back all side shoots to within 15 cm (6 in) of the main stems. Then, in late winter or early spring shorten them further, to two buds.

Other climbers   In general, thin out weak and congested growth in late winter or early spring. Tie in main stems to their supports.

HEDGES

For a good dense hedge you have to start training immediately after planting and in subsequent years carry out regular clipping (for formal hedges).

Training new hedges

Formal deciduous Reduce all growth to half or two-thirds of length (top and side shoots) after planting, in winter. This ensures dense growth at the base of the hedge.

Formal conifer and other evergreens Little pruning needed after planting – only cut back any over-long side shoots.

Informal hedges Cut back hard after planting, in winter, as for formal deciduous hedges.

Training in second and subsequent years

Formal deciduous Allow the ultimate height to be reached in stages. New growth of leading (top) shoots is reduced by half when it is between 20 and ·30 cm (8 and 12 in) long. Do this pruning in summer. Side shoots are cut back hard in winter.

Formal conifer and other evergreens Leading shoots are retained. If necessary trim back side shoots in late summer or winter, just to tidy them up. When the leading shoots are 15–30 cm (6–12 in) above the height you require for the hedge, reduce them to 15 cm (6 in) below the required height.

Informal hedges Leave them alone from now on, unless the side growth is sparse. In this case reduce leading shoots by half the length of the new growth. Do this in the second winter and, if necessary, again in the third winter. Then you will have a good dense hedge.

Regular trimming

After approximately three growing seasons regular trimming can start. For most hedging plants you can use garden shears or an electric hedge trimmer. For hedging plants which have very large leaves, like *Prunus laurocerasus* (laurel) cut individual shoots with secateurs. If you cut the large leaves in half they turn brown at the edges, which looks unsightly.

Formal hedges To ensure a straight top when trimming, place a garden line alone the top to indicate cutting height. Only trim the new growth lightly.

Some hedging plants, like ligustrum (privet), lonicera (Chinese honeysuckle) and buxus (box) need trimming several times during the growing season (mid-spring to late summer). Although box is comparatively slow growing it does need several trims to keep it looking neat and tidy.

Other formal hedges need cutting only once a year, in summer (not after late summer, though). The following are trimmed in late summer: carpinus (hornbeam), euonymus, fagus (beech), ilex (holly), and the conifers taxus (yew), chamaecyparis, × cupressocyparis, cupressus and thuja.

Informal hedges Only trim these to reduce in length any over-long or very straggly shoots. On no account trim the entire hedge. Use secateurs to cut back individual shoots and do this immediately after flowering.

ROSES

Some roses need regular pruning, others only occasional attention.

Large-flowered and cluster-flowered

Newly planted bushes should be cut back hard in early spring. All stems can be reduced to a height of 15 cm (6 in) above soil level. Remove any thin or spindly shoots. Routine pruning is carried out annually, also in early spring. Aim to produce an open-centred or cup-shaped bush consisting only of strong stems.

For large-flowered roses, the strong stems are cut back by half to two-thirds of their length; weaker ones to 5–8 cm (2–3 in). Remove completely very weak or spindly stems.

Cluster-flowered roses should have strong stems cut back by one-third to half their length; weaker ones by two-thirds. Again remove completely all very weak and spindly shoots.

Standard roses

Large-flowered and cluster-flowered standard roses are pruned as described above but ensure that all remaining branches are of the same length to give a symmetrical head.

Climbing roses

These are pruned in early spring. All the side shoots produced on the main stems are cut back to leave one to three growth buds.

Rambler roses

These are pruned immediately after flowering. Ramblers make new shoots near the base, which flower the following year. The old stems which have flowered are cut out completely and the new shoots tied in to their supports.

Other roses

The other groups of roses, like the shrub and species roses and ground-cover types, need no regular pruning, only the removal of any dead or extremely old wood.

PERENNIALS

Many modern herbaceous perennials support themselves, but others need staking, particularly tall kinds with thin stems and large flower heads, such as many asters or Michaelmas daisies. These can be supported by inserting twiggy sticks between and around the plants as they are starting into growth in the spring. The stems will then grow through these supports and hide them. They should be slightly below flowering height.

Some perennials produce several tall thick heavy flower spikes, such as delphiniums. Provide a stout bamboo cane for each stem before it becomes too tall.

Cut off dead flowers regularly, not only for the sake of tidiness, but also to encourage a second flush of blooms in some plants.

When the stems of herbaceous plants die back in autumn they should be cut down as close as possible to the crown of the plant. Evergreen perennials should have dead leaves removed as necessary.

Most perennials should be lifted and divided every three or four years to keep them young and vigorous. Some, though, should not be disturbed, and these include paeonias and kniphofias (red hot pokers). Others do not make clumps and so cannot be divided—for example, gypsophilia. Short-lived perennials, like lupins, are not divided, either.

INDEX

DATE DUE